WIN THE BATTLE AGAINST BURNOUT

*Created with love
by Forward Partners*

WIN THE BATTLE AGAINST BURNOUT

Reclaim the Three Elements that Trap You in Burnout

Chad Wright

Forward Publishing

ISBN: 979-8-9952253-0-0 (Paperback)

ISBN: 979-8-9952253-1-7 (eBook)

ISBN: 979-8-9952253-2-4 (Audiobook)

Library of Congress Control Number: 2026908825

This book is intended for informational and educational purposes only. The content is not a substitute for professional medical, psychological, or mental health advice, diagnosis, or treatment.

The author is not a licensed medical or mental health professional, and the views expressed in this book are based on personal experience, research, and opinion. Readers should consult a qualified healthcare provider or licensed mental health professional regarding any questions or concerns about their individual situation.

While every effort has been made to ensure the accuracy of the information presented, the author and publisher make no representations or warranties regarding the completeness, reliability, or applicability of the content. The use of any information provided in this book is solely at the reader's own risk.

If you are experiencing severe distress, mental health crisis, or thoughts of self-harm, please seek immediate assistance from a licensed professional or contact your local emergency services or a crisis hotline.

By reading this book, you acknowledge that the author and publisher are not responsible for any adverse effects or consequences resulting from the use of the information contained herein.

Edited by Elana Jackson
Front Cover and Book Design by Emily Deal
Illustrations by Calla Walshe
Photograph of the Author by Joe Fang

FIRST EDITION

Forward Publishing, LLC

P.O. Box 224
Leander, TX 78646

www.ForwardPartners.net

To order additional copies go to www.BattleBurnout.net.
For bulk order discounts, email books@forwardpartners.net.

To my parents, Allan and Connie,
for their unwavering belief.

To my wife, Rebecca, for never giving up
on me, in spite of everything.

To my sons, Colton, Conner, and Cody,
for being honorable men.

I love you all.

CONTENTS

PART 3: ESCAPING THE TRAP

PART 4: MOVING FORWARD

HUSTLE
JUICE

INTRODUCTION

"This isn't working," Rebecca said.

Her words echoed in my soul, and despite my best efforts, tears began to run down my cheeks. Shame kept my eyes locked to the floor because I could no longer hide the despair I was feeling. When I finally found the strength to look across the porch at my wife and parents, they reflected my despair back at me.

"This isn't working," Rebecca repeated quietly.

I tried to respond, but my words were choked off before they could even leave my mouth. Inside my mind, I screamed and railed against the reality I had created. *Of course, this isn't working! And I don't know how to fix it!*

They stared at me, hoping to hear words I didn't have.

It was the fall of 2010, and I was five years into owning a business. From the outside, it probably looked like I was doing my best to go out of business, even though inside I was doing all I could to keep the doors open. In my quest to find success, I did the only thing I knew to do: I worked hard. When that didn't bear fruit, I worked harder. In fact, that was my answer to everything: *Just work harder!*

The "freedom" I had sought in owning my own business evaporated in the crucible of eighty-hour work weeks. Almost every day turned into a fourteen-hour day. *Just one more task*, I'd tell myself, not realizing it was 10:30 p.m. and the entire family had gone to bed. "I just need to finish this project," I'd explain to my young family on a Saturday afternoon, when they wanted to go to the park. Wash, rinse, repeat. *Just work harder.*

That cycle continued until I landed on my parents' back porch, intervention-style, with three sets of eyes pleading with me to see the truth. My wife and parents had everything except handwritten notes explaining how my actions had hurt them. *Maybe I do need an intervention*, I thought. *I've created all this pain*. My marriage and family life were teetering on the brink of disaster.

Our bank account was empty.

Our best friend was overdraft protection.

Our credit cards were maxed out.

Our relationships were at rock bottom.

Our kids needed a father who wasn't always angry.

I was broke and felt completely broken, and I could not understand how things had gotten so bad. I was raised with a simple adage: If you work hard enough, you can do anything. But I *had* worked hard — harder than I had in my entire life. And yet, I could barely make ends meet.

At the time, I thought the "This" in "This isn't working" was money. More precisely, the *lack* of money. It would take me several more years to learn that "This" was actually burnout. I was so burned out that I no longer had the capacity to show up in a positive way in any area of my life. Because of burnout, I had abandoned my own health, ignored my family's true needs, and failed to do anything that would bring growth to my business.

While the adage I was raised with is true, it is also incomplete. If you work hard enough, you can do anything — *until you break*. In those three simple words ("until you break") is an acknowledgment of the finite nature of humans. We are limited, and we do have breaking points. I was in the middle of crashing so spectacularly into a breaking point that I could see important parts of my life shearing off and flying in all directions. I was just learning that I was in a war with burnout, yet I felt like I had already lost completely.

I sat there, on that back porch, surrounded by people who only wanted good for me. And yet, I felt alone. If I acknowledged that I was this weak, would my wife and parents believe I could claw us back from the edge? Or would they give up on me? Even as I write this, I feel deep compassion for the thirty-year-old me. The thought that *I* had to single-handedly bring the family back from the brink seems so silly now. But back then, this thinking was my reality. I felt *I* had to fix everything. I was backed by a smart, supportive, and loving team, yet I had completely isolated myself. I was driven by a need to prove that I was strong enough to make it all work *on my own*.

Why couldn't my younger self know what I know now? Because I needed to break in order to learn. In fact, I would need to hit a few other breaking points along the way to learn just how much of my life burnout was destroying, and just how much I needed other people.

I would live and relive a pattern over the next few years. Any sign of financial challenge would cause me to go back to my muscle memory: *Just work harder*. They were the strongest muscles I had, so in each crisis, I would flex them. Day after day, I worked harder and harder, until burnout, once again, chipped away at any joy in my life.

My conversations with Rebecca became shorter and angrier.

My three sons became a source of annoyance rather than joy.

I isolated myself from everyone.

Then, again, I would hear the same words, "This isn't working." Sometimes the message came from within myself. Often it came from my family, which was even more infuriating. *Don't they see I'm doing all this for them?*

But I wasn't doing it for them. Not really. I was doing it for my ego. I was doing it to quiet my fears of inadequacy and to serve the unreasonable and unachievable expectations I had placed on myself. I was doing it to prove that I was *enough*. I remained locked in the cycle of burnout — until I learned that hard work alone wasn't the answer.

Three things changed that eventually broke this pattern: First, I got help. I was finally able to raise my hand and admit I needed help. This led to finding counselors, coaches, and mentors who would alter the course of my life. Then, I began to study burnout and leadership. And finally, I began to take action, internalizing everything I was learning and turning it into daily practices.

Through engagement with very smart people, constant study on the subject of burnout, and intentional action, I started to change. I began, for perhaps the first time in my life, to truly lead. I learned to lead myself first so that I could then effectively lead others. This meant establishing daily practices around my own leadership health, and honoring the rhythms that my mind, body, and soul were designed for.

As I progressed on this journey, I began to feel healthier, and I started to see outcomes in my life changing. I found success, not by sheer force, but by intentional design. I began to realize that healthy leadership is at the heart of winning the battle against burnout. When I show up as a healthy leader, I am capable of creating incredibly positive impact. When I am unintentional, however, I default to my old ways of thinking and acting. Healthy leadership is at the heart of the success we are *all* seeking.

If leadership is the answer then we need to better train leaders. As I looked around at the people in my life, I noticed that all my friends were CEOs or pastors. All of them were experiencing burnout, and I could see the negative effect it was having on them, their families, and the organizations they were leading. Despite living in a world overflowing with leadership authors, speakers, and trainers, there are still a lot of leaders who are losing the battle against burnout.

I was determined to see if I could find a way to tackle this problem. I hired my friend Terry Ishee to come in and help me think through what I wanted to teach leaders. Terry is a phenomenal teacher and coach in his own right. We would sit, one day each week, with a blank whiteboard. Over the course of those months, we sketched out the beginnings of what I wanted to spend my life doing and teaching.

On August 28, 2018, I launched my coaching firm, Forward Partners. I gave my first talk on healthy leadership, burnout, and purpose at a luncheon for the Leander Chamber of Commerce in Leander, Texas. When I stepped off the stage, the first person to greet me was Bridget Brandt, the president of the chamber. She gave me a hug and said, "Why haven't you written a book yet?" That question has been pinging around my brain for the past seven years. I always knew I would write a book (much to the disbelief of every English teacher I've ever had), but what I didn't know was how much more experience I would need before I could write something helpful.

We've spent the past seven years deploying these ideas about healthy leadership, burnout, and thriving teams within many organizations. Each time we begin with a new organization, I know two things to be true: First, if they are willing to do the work, their lives will change for the better. And second, *I* am going to learn something new. The foundation of what we believe and teach goes all the way back to the whiteboards Terry and I filled up. The specifics, however, evolve with each new engagement. Each time I learn something new, it makes our work that much more impactful.

Through this work, though, I keep running into a common problem. Very smart people look at the tools we provide — the tools to win the battle against burnout — and say, "I should use these," but then they don't use them. Why? Why can we acknowledge intellectually that using these tools is wise, but when push comes to shove, we revert to our old muscle memory that led to burnout in the first place? Why do we continue to lose a winnable battle?

That is what I needed another seven years to learn. Had I written this book even a year ago, it would have been about the tools themselves. It would have been what we teach in our workshops, retreats, and training, all wrapped up nicely in book form. And while it would have been great (and might be a companion to this book in the future), it wouldn't have spoken to the core question we're wrestling with: Why do smart people refuse to do the simple things needed to win the battle against burnout?

You see, winning the battle against burnout involves very simple tools — they are easy to both understand and implement. Unfortunately, we are the ones who have to implement them, and while the tools are insanely simple, *we are insanely complex.* We are the sum total of every experience we've had up to this point. That means each of us is a wild jumble of experiences, stories, fear, shame, opinions, and anxiety. It's like we're dealing with a giant ball of impossibly tangled Christmas lights. We have to find a way to straighten it all out before we can hope to put it on the tree.

Through this book and this work, you'll discover how early messages of shame can skew our view of our identity, causing us to take on unsustainable expectations and then judge ourselves as broken. Those three elements — identity, expectations, and judgment — conspire to keep us trapped in burnout. This perpetuates a cycle of burnout in each of our lives, causing us to overpromise, overcommit, and overwork, all at the cost of the life we deserve and the impact we're meant to have. You will learn to take intentional action, to implement regular practices to show up in your life as a healthy leader and win the battle against burnout each day.

The week I wrote this, I was blessed to officiate the wedding of my son Conner to his amazing bride Emily. As we celebrated throughout that day, there were so many moments when I was reminded how incredible life is. I walked down the aisle with Conner, pointing out the beauty of the setting sun flashing through the trees. I watched as the bride and groom struggled through tears and laughter to read their vows. As I conducted the service, I looked across the crowd at Rebecca and saw the joy in her eyes.

There was one moment, though, that really stood out. During the reception, all three of my sons came walking down a grand staircase, all sporting tuxedos with black silk bow ties. The pride and love I felt overwhelmed me. I thought back to that moment on the cold back porch in late 2010. The younger version of me had *no idea* what he could lose. As I watched them descend those stairs, I realized that my work to win the battle against burnout was about so much more than just me and my health. I saw the future potential of my three sons and their families, and I knew my work would echo long into the future. *This battle is worth winning, and this war is worth fighting.* Not just for me and my family, but for leaders everywhere. In that moment, I became more determined than ever to do this work.

I want my sons, and everyone reading this book, to learn from my mistakes and take advantage of everything that resonates. *Do not let burnout win this battle.*

I am not Moses coming down from on high with tablets saying, "*You* should do this!" I'm right alongside you on the same journey. Each day, I get up and do the mindset work necessary to keep moving forward. Each day, I have to choose to use the tools that result in healthy leadership. Each day, I have to remind myself that I am enough. Each day, I have to embrace my ability to create the future. I'm shoulder to shoulder with you, saying "*We* have to do this."

We owe it to everyone who loves us.

We owe it to everyone who looks to us for leadership.

We owe it to *ourselves*.

American philosopher Howard Thurman said, "Don't ask what the world needs. Ask what makes you come alive, and go do it. Because what the world needs is people who have come alive."

It's time to come alive.

Let's go.

Part 1

THE ENEMY

"If you know
your enemy and
know yourself,
you need not fear
the result of a
hundred battles."

— Sun Tzu,
The Art of War

Chapter 1

KNOW YOUR ENEMY

You are fighting, and most likely losing, an unwinnable war. "Wait!" I can hear you say. "The cover of this book says *Win the Battle Against Burnout*. What do you mean 'an unwinnable war'? I want my money back." Just stick with me; it'll all make sense by the end of this chapter.

Our enemy in this war is burnout. It stalks us relentlessly, watching each of our choices, finding ways to insert itself between us and true success. It knows our weaknesses better than we do. It feeds on our ego and fear, using them to keep us trapped. It knows that if we stay trapped long enough, we will give up. In giving up, we suffer the ultimate defeat: the loss of our potential impact.

Let's start this journey off with some honesty. Every time someone like Simon Sinek or Brené Brown releases a book, we purchase it simply because their name is on the cover. I know I do. You most likely *did not* pick this book up because it said "by Chad Wright" on the cover. That's okay.

The real reason you picked it up was because it had the word BURNOUT emblazoned across the front, as large and as bold as we could possibly make it. Even now, when you read the word burnout, you can *feel* it. It's a tightness in your chest. It's a never-ending weight of responsibilities and tasks bearing down on you. It's an inability to fully breathe out. It's a lack of peace.

Burnout was first discussed in 1974 by psychotherapist Herbert Freudenberger.[1] Since then, it has become a part of our everyday language. More than just a part of our vocabulary, though, it has become a shared experience.

Burnout has spread at an unrelenting pace because our society is a machine built to generate "success." We've learned over time that the more effort we put into the machine, the more success it creates. We've also discovered that the success it generates is not enough. It never will be. Our society is driven by a few keywords: More. Bigger. Newer. Faster. This infinite striving makes our society great (we can imagine and create anything!), but it's also burning us out. We are the fuel for the machine, and we are not infinite beings. Each day, we wrestle with the limits of our capacity.

Unfortunately, like with any machine, there is the primary output and then there are byproducts. A byproduct of our machine is burnout. When we burn out, we are replaced with a fresh model and the machine continues to turn. This is all well and good for the machine, but what about the people being tossed aside like empty batteries?

I know this sounds dramatic, but we see it happen all the time. People serve for thirty or forty years in their career. They begin their journey with vibrance and excitement, energy and purpose. By the end, we are all clapping at their retirement party, not because we're proud of them, but because we're glad we don't have to work with them anymore. They have burned out to the point where they are a husk of their former selves. They are bitter, short-tempered, micromanagers. *Thank the Lord we no longer have to sit next to them in the Monday morning update meetings.*

This is not an uncommon occurrence. I know because I make

that joke all the time when I'm speaking at conferences. I ask if everyone is picturing a specific person in their minds, and they laugh and nod their heads yes. We have all experienced those coworkers. Some of us *are* those coworkers sometimes.

From the introduction of the idea of burnout in 1974 to today, burnout has become an epidemic. *Forbes* recently reported that sixty-six percent of workers surveyed reported experiencing burnout at work.[2] The spread of burnout has become so pervasive that in 2019, it became an actual medical diagnosis. Not just a feeling, it is now a syndrome. The World Health Organization (WHO), in its handbook the *ICD-11*, defines burnout in the following way:

> *Burnout is a syndrome conceptualized as resulting from chronic workplace stress that has not been successfully managed. It is characterised by three dimensions: 1) feelings of energy depletion or exhaustion; 2) increased mental distance from one's job, or feelings of negativism or cynicism related to one's job; and 3) a sense of ineffectiveness and lack of accomplishment. Burnout refers specifically to phenomena in the occupational context and should not be applied to describe experiences in other areas of life.*[3]

I'm glad we are beginning to treat burnout as the serious problem it is (and if burnout is affecting your physical and mental health in noticeable ways, then *please seek out professional help*). However, I'm not a big fan of the WHO's definition for two reasons: One, burnout is not caused exclusively by our work. Two, the effects of burnout are not contained at work. It's not as though our brains look at stress coming from home and say, "That's home stress, so I won't add it to the mountain of work stress causing my burnout." It's also not as though we can walk through the front door of our homes and have all the effects of burnout magically evaporate, like a morning mist when the sun rises.

The burnout epidemic has to be viewed more holistically for us to find solutions. Burnout can come from any area of our lives, and it infects every area of our lives. Many books about burnout focus on the work aspect only, and some even put the responsibility for a solution solely on the organization. While there is wisdom to be found in some of those books, I don't agree with the above ideas. They remove the agency *we all have* to take action to defeat burnout. They also ignore our own role in sustaining and spreading burnout.

Redefining Burnout

To guide us on this journey, I've written a different definition of burnout. Anytime you see the word burnout in this book, this is the definition I am referencing:

———

Burnout is the loss of capacity to align with your purpose, do your most sacred work, and enjoy life.

———

Burnout robs us of the capacity to live the life we are meant to live. It keeps us trapped on a hamster wheel of false productivity. We are not meant for a hamster wheel. We are meant to show up every day, have a positive impact in every area of our life, and to do so sustainably. For burnout to sustain itself, it must destroy access to our purpose, sacred work, and joy.

Purpose

Our purpose is the way we were designed to impact this world. We are each here to have a positive impact through service to others. We do that in a way that is uniquely *us*. That one-of-a-kind mix of talents, skills, and personality define what we are capable of when we are at our best. Truly living out our purpose requires us to show up at our best — bringing those skills and talents to bear to make other people's lives better in ways both big and small.

Our ability to live out our purpose is hampered when we are trapped in burnout. When burnout takes over, it is hard to show up fully aligned with our purpose because we're just trying to show up *at all*. That means we are unable to bring the best version of ourselves to serve everyone we lead and influence. This robs everyone around us of the positive impact we could be having, and it robs us of the realization that we matter.

Sacred Work

We are meant to do sacred work. For each person, that work is different. For many of us, it's parenting and building families. In addition to that, many of us have a calling to the professional work we do every day. You might be thinking, "I am not *called* to look at spreadsheets." Maybe not. But hear me out — what if you *are*? I believe that almost all work can be tied to some positive impact on other people. That makes it important work, and I would even argue, *sacred* work. The spreadsheets might not feel special, but the impact we have on others through our work with spreadsheets is.

The word sacred can carry religious connotations. We often think of priests, pastors, and missionaries as doing sacred work. However, there is a definition of sacred that is "worthy of respect and dedication."[4] When we do things that are in service to others, we are doing something worthy of respect and dedication. We are doing sacred work.

Burnout will cause us to lose touch with the impact we are capable of having on the people around us and decrease our capacity to do that sacred work.

Joy

We are here to enjoy life. *Burnout hates joy*. Burnout hates contentment and peace. Burnout hates rest. But all these things can be found. When we loosen the grip burnout has on our lives, we can slow down and see life for what it really is — magical.

One of the greatest regrets of my life is that I rarely enjoyed my sons when they were small. Because I was so burned out, and my world was all about *me*, I was always waiting for what was next, hoping it might be easier. I didn't look at my two-year-old and see the magic of a tiny version of me learning to navigate the world. No, I looked at him and wanted to know when he would be able to wipe his own butt because I had better things to do. I didn't look at them at age five and marvel at the fact that they were about to begin a new adventure by going to school. I looked at them and wondered when they were going to start driving because I was tired of carting them around.

On the other hand, when I watched my grown sons walk down the staircase together at the wedding, I wasn't thinking about any of the frustrations we'd had when they were young, or how annoying they'd been as teenagers (spoiler alert: super annoying). Instead, it was all I could do to keep tears of joy from flowing. It was a reminder to experience joy in the moment, but it was also about all the joy I had missed when burnout had reigned supreme.

Life is about joy in monumental moments like that, and small moments as well. As I write these words, I'm sitting outside at Tequilo's Tex-Mex in Galveston, Texas. I just enjoyed the most incredible lunch and am basking in the sunny, sixty-five-degree day. I feel peace and joy.

From big moments to small, burnout has us so focused on what's wrong, we can't see how blessed we *really* are.

When we show up at our best and do sacred work, we will find joy — unless burnout wins the daily battle. The war with burnout will never end. From the moment of first consciousness to the moment we breathe our last breath, burnout will be plotting and taking action, hellbent on our destruction. So why fight? Each day when we wake up, possibly wounded and battle weary from the days before, we have one undeniable gift — we have another day to fight. To fight not just against burnout, but to fight *for* something. To fight for our family. To fight for a lasting marriage. To fight for our children's future. To fight for our team. To fight for the impact of our work.

To fight for a better world.

While the war against burnout will never end, the battle each day *can be won*. Burnout can be routed. It can be outflanked, outmaneuvered, and outclassed. Each day is a new chance to fight and win. As we learn to do the work and win the daily battle against burnout, we will increase our capacity to live the life we are meant to live, having the impact we are meant to have.

CHAPTER 1 REFLECTION

Reflection Questions

1. Have you ever felt like burnout was stopping you from pursuing something you were called to do?

....

....

....

....

....

....

2. Describe a time when burnout robbed you of the ability to *enjoy* your life.

....

....

....

....

....

....

3. How do you think your life would look if burnout wasn't
    stealing your capacity?

....

....

....

....

....

....

....

Take Action

Winning the battle against burnout eventually requires help from
others. We'll cover that thoroughly later in this book. For now,
begin to think about who you can ask to join you on this journey
and write down their names. If you're feeling extra generous, send
them a copy of this book. ;-)

CHAPTER 1 ENDNOTES

1. Herbert Freudenberger, "Staff Burn-Out" (Journal of Social Issues, 1974), 30:159-65.

2. Bryan Robinson, PhD, "Job Burnout At 66% in 2025, New Study Shows" (Forbes, 2025), https://www.forbes.com/sites/bryanrobinson/2025/02/08/job-burnout-at-66-in-2025-new-study-shows/.

3. World Health Organization, *ICD-11 for Mortality and Morbidity Statistics* (WHO, 2025), QD85, https://icd.who.int/browse/2025-01/mms/en#129180281.

4. Vocabulary.com, https://www.vocabulary.com/dictionary/sacred.

"My one purpose in life is to serve as a warning to others."

— Jamie Zawinski,
Computer Programmer

Chapter 2

SIGNS OF BURNOUT

NOPE

By the time I made it to The Back Porch Intervention (as I'll call it going forward), I had been outwardly exhibiting the classic signs of burnout. However, despite displaying all of them, I was usually unaware of them. That's because burnout is, if you'll excuse the pun, often a slow burn.

As author Jennifer Moss says in her book, *The Burnout Epidemic: The Rise of Chronic Stress and How We Can Fix It*, "Burnout isn't something that just happens overnight. It's a slow erosion of coping skills and one's ability to adapt to the daily chronic stress that finally overwhelms."[1]

It's not a sudden weight that crushes us but a steady accumulation of stress and damage that eventually becomes too much to bear. Because of the slow creep of burnout, the signs are not always apparent in the moment. Unfortunately, they are there, draining our capacity, chipping away at our relationships, and strangling our hope.

Burnout is often characterized by a consistent sense of overwhelm, fatigue, cynicism, and loneliness. As we illustrate these four main symptoms, I want you to think about your life as it is today, and see how many symptoms you can recognize in yourself.

Overwhelm

Overwhelm is best characterized as a loss of proper perspective. A consistent sense of overwhelm is a sign of burnout. You can tell you are overwhelmed when small problems cause big reactions. Overwhelm tells you, "This isn't a small problem, this is a GIANT problem. And this problem will wreck everything!" Cue the mushroom cloud in your head.

Parents of toddlers know exactly how this feels. You warn a toddler not to run around the table because she is going to spill the milk that's sitting on the table. The toddler, clearly on a mission to ruin your entire life, barrels around the corner of the table as fast as her little legs will carry her.

"Stop running around the table; you are going to knock the milk over!" you implore her, more exasperated this time.

On the fourth circuit, her shoulder clips the edge, rocking the table. You watch as, in slow motion, the cup teeters on the edge. The milk pours over the lip of the cup and plunges toward the ground. The cup bounces on the floor, each impact mocking your frustration. The milk is now spreading across your previously clean floor at a leisurely pace.

Your daughter, the light of your life, stares at you with her best look of angelic innocence. You can literally feel the pressure building. From the tip of your toes, it rapidly moves up your body, seeking a release.

I told her she was going to spill the milk, and now she spilled the milk, and now I have to stop and clean up the milk, which means mopping the floors, which means I'm going to be late for my Zoom call with the finance director, and he is going to hate my being late, which will put him in a bad mood, which means he'll be cranky and probably say something to piss me off, and I'll just have to take it because I was late to the meeting — BECAUSE OF THE MILK!

Finally, that pressure shoves aside your commitment to gentle parenting and finds a release point, up through your throat and out of your mouth. With a crimson red face, you let loose a string of obscenities that would make a sailor run away. Three weeks later, when your angel uses the f-word for the first time in front of your mother-in-law, you'll flash back to this moment.

Now, is it hard to clean up milk? No.

Small problem. Big reaction. Overwhelm.

This isn't a problem felt exclusively at home either. The meeting has gone an hour over schedule, and the boss asks if anyone has any further questions. *Of course no one has any more questions,* you think. *What idiot would have more questions?*

Carl's hand eagerly shoots up into the air.

You scream in your head, *Dammit, Carl. No! The answer is no! No, you don't have any more questions!*

Carl begins speaking, and you slam your laptop shut with enough force to cause every pen to rattle, and every head to turn your way. *Can they not see how much I have to do?*

You stare at them all, equal parts embarrassed and angry.

Carl problem. Big reaction. Overwhelm.

Your perspective is not the only thing affected by overwhelm. As your frustration builds, your fuse shortens, and your sharp edges start to come out. Now people around you are experiencing a version of you that is unintentionally doing damage.

The loss of perspective also causes a loss of valuable productivity. When everything seems like an emergency, it's hard to discern the truly important work that needs to be done. A variety of different demands all seem to be pulling you in different directions. This can often lead to a feeling of spinning your wheels. You can check a thousand tasks off the list today, but who knows if any of them really matter. It proves the old adage true — when everything is a priority, nothing is a priority. Progress is hard to measure when your life seems like a never-ending stream of massive challenges, and overwhelm ensures that life *always* seems that way.

Fatigue

How often do you go to bed tired and wake up just as tired? Start your weekend tired and finish your weekend tired? Fatigue is an easy one to explain because it is so common. It's not just *being* tired, it's the inability to *overcome* your tiredness. Your capacity to find rest is diminished because you are *always* on the go, seemingly just existing from stopping point to stopping point. From the moment you wake up to the moment you lie down again, you are always *doing* something — usually in the name of productivity. But rarely are you able to enjoy a sense that you've accomplished anything. Meanwhile, this rhythm drains your capacity to experience anything good, including rest.

You wake up on Saturday morning, having slept *all* the way until 6:00 a.m. The room fills with the smell of freshly brewed coffee. From the kitchen window, you see the beautiful sunrise, the dawn of a new weekend. You look down at your full coffee cup and smile to yourself. *It's going to be a great weekend.*

Looking back out the window, you are surprised to find the rising sun has been replaced with a setting sun. You look down at your hand again, and the coffee cup has been replaced with a rocks glass and two fingers of scotch. Not even the good stuff. The good stuff is for Friday evening. It's for celebration. But this is ... *Sunday evening? How did this happen?* It felt like you just woke up. *What happened to the weekend?* Weren't you going to slow down and enjoy these two days?

Unfortunately, rest isn't something you magically stumble into, especially when you are already operating with high levels of fatigue. Fatigue lowers your capacity to be truly productive and also makes it harder to find true rest. The times you do get to sit down, you may find yourself mindlessly scrolling through Netflix, trying to find something to watch. After an hour of flipping through shows you'll never watch, you give up in defeat and pick up your phone. Now you're scrolling through Instagram, sucked into the never-ending rabbit hole of Reels, video after video of people doing *really* dumb things. That time ends up being numbing but not restful, and it contributes to even higher levels of fatigue.

Most people experiencing fatigue usually operate with an I-just-need-to-survive-until-vacation mentality. In their overflowing calendars, there are only two or three blocks of empty space throughout the year. There is one word protecting that space: vacation. Unfortunately, the same inability to find rest in the evening or over the weekend can persist through vacation as well.

In a later chapter, I'll talk about the rhythms of rest, but the short version is this: If you don't honor the daily or weekly rhythms of rest that you are designed to *need*, no vacation on the planet will solve your fatigue problems.

The amount of activity you engage in is one challenge that adds to fatigue, but so are the inputs and distractions you encounter every day. The longer you spend in the state of overwhelm we discussed in the last section, the lower is your capacity to process inputs.

Technology has made it infinitely easier to communicate, but it also leads to a quantity over quality mindset. You are overwhelmed by endless texts, emails, social media posts, Zoom calls, Facetime calls, and even good old-fashioned *phone* calls. Additionally, every social media platform has its own separate messaging component. You're in a losing battle with those little red notification circles, always trying to reduce the numbers to zero. None of this takes into account all the in-person inputs you experience each day. It's enough to make you yearn for the days of smoke signals. Your world is one of overwhelming inputs and a nagging feeling of always being behind. The sheer number of inputs you experience leads to a consistent feeling of fatigue. When you're in an ongoing state of fatigue, your capacity is greatly diminished and rest is increasingly elusive.

Cynicism

I am, admittedly, a naturally cynical person. Usually, this quality manifests in a lot of sarcasm. So how can you tell if we're talking burnout-grade cynicism versus normal levels of snark? The type of cynicism we're talking about here is the kind in which a person can take literally any good thing that happens and tell you why it is, in fact, bad. It's the type of mindset in which seemingly nothing will ever be good enough. It's also the kind of cynicism that is highly contagious. A person infected with this type of cynicism walks around with it dripping from every word they say. Negativity seems to ooze out of their pores.

You are feeling great today. You turn to leave the breakroom, steaming cup of coffee in hand. Blocking your path is *Carl*. He strolls through the doorway, the stench of suffocating negativity preceding him into the room.

    Don't engage. Don't engage. Don't engage.

    Carl shuffles by you, and you pray his zombie-like gaze doesn't fall on you. You turn to quietly exit the room.

    "So ...," he says as a preamble. You are frozen in place by his single word.

    "I heard they are giving us an eight percent raise this year," Carl continues. "Something about inflation, so they are paying us more than the usual cost-of-living adjustment."

Wait, did Carl just say something positive?

"Uh, yeah," you say tentatively, unsure how to proceed.

Carl's dull eyes turn from his tea to you, locking you in place. He audibly inhales a deep breath, and you envision toxic green vapor wafting around his head.

"Well, let me tell you," he says, "I spent the weekend digging through the financial reports of the company, and they can afford a *lot* more than an eight percent raise. In fact, it should have been closer to fifteen percent. As usual, they're taking advantage of us. The CEO said she was going to forgo her raise this year to help fund our additional percentage points, but we know that's just for show. Plus, have you seen where she lives? She isn't giving up anything. We should all protest. Eight percent? You know, my friend works for our competitor. He says it's great over there. We should all leave. Eight percent? It's insulting. After all we do for this company, that's all they could scrounge out of their vaults. Don't you just hate it here?"

Mouth agape, you are unable to respond to the tirade of cynicism you were just assaulted with. Carl, believing he has just done a great service by opening your eyes to the *injustice* of an eight percent raise, calmly gathers up his mug of tea and strides out of the room.

Now you stand alone, in a dirty break room. *Was it this dirty when I walked in here?* Somehow, the lights are now dull and flickering, giving the tile floor a sickening yellow-green hue. You take a sip of your now lukewarm coffee and your face registers disgust. You shuffle out of the room, mumbling quietly to yourself, "Only eight percent? Maybe I do hate it here."

One conversation with Carl, and you went from being an engaged, optimistic, productive employee to Milton Waddams from *Office Space* threatening to "burn the building down" because someone took your red stapler.

Cynicism, when it's fueled by burnout, ensures that you are unable to see the bright side of *anything*. This is where the concept of a "self-fulfilling prophecy" comes in, and burnout recruits your brain to work against you. Your brain is designed to give off a hit of dopamine — the pleasure chemical — whenever it finds what it is looking for or makes a new discovery. Therefore, whatever story your brain is looking for, that is the reality you will see because then your brain gets to give itself that hit of sweet, sweet dopamine. It doesn't even matter what reality is. If cynicism tells you that everything is terrible, then your brain will be wired to see confirmation of how terrible things are so it can be rewarded.

In this sense, your brain is like a drug-addicted liar that prevents you from seeing truth. Cynicism leads to a self-perpetuating loop by being a self-fulfilling prophecy. When you believe the story that everything is bad, no matter how good things really are, your brain will twist reality to show you the dark side. When you see the dark side, your brain says, "SEE, I was right! I'll take that dopamine, thank you." That's the self-perpetuating loop. Brain believes story. Brain shows you that reality. Brain feels goooood.

This is also where you end up being a big part of the problem without realizing that you are. Your subconscious determines the version of you that shows up each day. When you are unintentional about choosing which version, it simply uses whatever story it currently has in its programming to choose. If that story is "Everything is bad," it will create a version of you that *actually contributes* to everything being bad. You become a big part of the very problem you will decry.

Carl believes he is the hero of the story, not the problem. But the reality is, Carl is doing a huge disservice to himself and everyone around him. When burnout fuels your cynicism, there are times when you show up, and you *are* Carl.

But there is hope! In later chapters, we'll explore how

"disempowered stories" drive our brains, and we'll do the work of rewriting these stories. This will allow you to choose how you see and experience the world — keeping cynicism from dominating your life.

Loneliness

Loneliness is the playground where burnout does its most insidious work. You look around at the perfectly curated social media profiles and believe everyone has it together. *They* are able to juggle the infinite demands of a successful career, care for their growing family (all in matching holiday pajamas), and somehow show up to the gym each day. *Why can't I do that?*

Burnout whispers to you that you are the only one who struggles. To admit that you struggle would be to open yourself up to ridicule. People would see just how weak you are, and then what would happen? People would know that you don't have it all figured out, and sometimes just making it through the day is a challenge.

This creates a cycle in which burnout convinces you that vulnerability is weakness, so you isolate yourself from others, hiding the truth. *Because you are isolated*, your burnout becomes more severe. The worse it gets, the more you isolate yourself. Again — wash, rinse, repeat. So much of burnout is experienced in repeated cycles. All the while, you are fooled into thinking you are doing things the right way. You've been taught, after all, that leadership is lonely. A lonely leader *must* be a good leader.

Well then, at the depths of my burnout, I must have been the *greatest* leader ever, because I was *so* alone. The core fear of my personality type is a fear of being inadequate. I'm constantly looking around for signs that people have realized that I don't measure up. When I was trapped in the darkest seasons of burnout, I desperately needed help from others. In fact, help from others was the *only* way I would ever get out of burnout. But to admit that I needed help would be to confirm my deepest fear — that I was inadequate. Every challenge that popped up became one more burden I had to shoulder by myself.

When no one was around, I would find some dramatic movie score and turn it up, loud enough to rattle the walls. I would sit, alone, and cry. Not crying with a singular tear falling down my cheek as I stared dramatically off into the distance. No, it was the type of crying that involved my whole body shaking as I curled up into the fetal position, shedding uncontrollable tears mixed with snot. So much snot. I secretly hoped someone would find me there, curled up on the floor. Then there would be no denying that I needed help. I would be found out, the Band-Aid ripped off in one instant. But no one found me.

I wept alone.

I did not know how to utter the three simple words that would have solved *everything*:

"I need help."

We all dread saying those words because we think people will see us as weak. They will see us as frauds who have been pretending we have it all together. Spoiler alert: WE ARE ALL PRETENDING! *Anyone* who claims to have it all figured out has not lived long enough for life to demonstrate just how much they don't know. The truth is, we are all showing up each day and doing the best we can.

Not only that, but when we have the courage and strength to say "I need help" (yes, this is *true* courage and strength), something magical happens: Instead of mocking us with disdain, people show up to help. That simple phrase opens up so many doors. It reveals a world of resources, an abundance, that we can tap into through other people. If you have ever said those three words and not received help, you just haven't said them to the right people. Don't give up on the power of raising your hand and asking for help.

We need other people. We are not meant to navigate life alone. U.S. Surgeon General Vivek Murthy sounded the alarm about loneliness in a 2023 Health and Human Services Advisory, calling loneliness an *epidemic*. "Lacking social connection can increase the risk for premature death as much as smoking up to 15 cigarettes a day."[2] My parents were quick to warn me about the dangers of smoking. No one told me that being a loner was just as dangerous.

If you find yourself trapped in loneliness and either don't have anyone to reach out to, or can't find the strength to do it, there are resources available. The 988 Suicide and Crisis Lifeline is one of those resources. As their website says, "Whether you're facing mental health struggles, emotional distress, alcohol or drug use concerns, or just need someone to talk to, our caring counselors are here for you. You are not alone."[3]

Burnout knows that when we're isolated, we will remain trapped, so it will continue to whisper lies in our ears. Every day that we refuse to embrace healthy vulnerability and refuse to embrace the help of other people, we are *choosing* burnout. We are choosing the seductively whispered *lie* that has us sitting in the depths of burnout. "You're strong," it says. "But only if you stay quiet. Figure it out on your own. You want to be strong, don't you?"

Nothing good begins with a lie.

The Burnout Checklist

As we went through the four major signs of burnout, you may have said, "Check, check, check, check." It wasn't exactly a list we wanted to complete, but here we are. We are all susceptible to overwhelm, fatigue, cynicism, and loneliness. The severity of these signs and symptoms can rise and fall on a moment-to-moment basis, but anyone who is experiencing burnout will probably recognize all four in some part of their lives. The good news is, if you can spot any of the four signs of burnout in your life, then you have taken the first step in doing something about it. You can take intentional action to win the battle against burnout. The next intentional action is to keep reading.

CHAPTER 2 REFLECTION

Reflection Questions

1. How many of the four common signs of burnout can you recognize in your life? Write an example of each.

2. Think of an example where overwhelm skewed your perspective on a situation. What kind of reaction did the overwhelm generate? Did that reaction cause damage to yourself or others?

3. If you spot yourself trapped in overwhelm or cynicism, who is
    that person you can reach out to for proper perspective?

....

....

....

....

....

....

Take Action

If you recognize loneliness in your life, reach out to *someone*. I
promise you that you are not alone. Reach out to others and open
up about how you are doing. You will find the help you need to
solve the loneliness problem.

CHAPTER 2 ENDNOTES

1. Jennifer Moss, *The Burnout Epidemic: The Rise of Chronic Stress and How We Can Fix It* (Harvard Business Review Press, 2021), 17.

2. Vivek Murthy, "Our Epidemic of Loneliness and Isolation: The U.S. Surgeon General's Advisory on the Healing Effects of Social Connection and Community" (U.S. Department of Health and Human Services, 2023), 9, https://www.hhs.gov/sites/default/files/surgeon-general-social-connection-advisory.pdf.

3. The 988 Suicide & Crisis Lifeline, https://988lifeline.org/.

"Success is not
final, failure is
not fatal: it is
the courage to
continue that
counts."

— Winston Churchill

Chapter 3

THE BURNOUT CURVE

THE BURNOUT CURVE

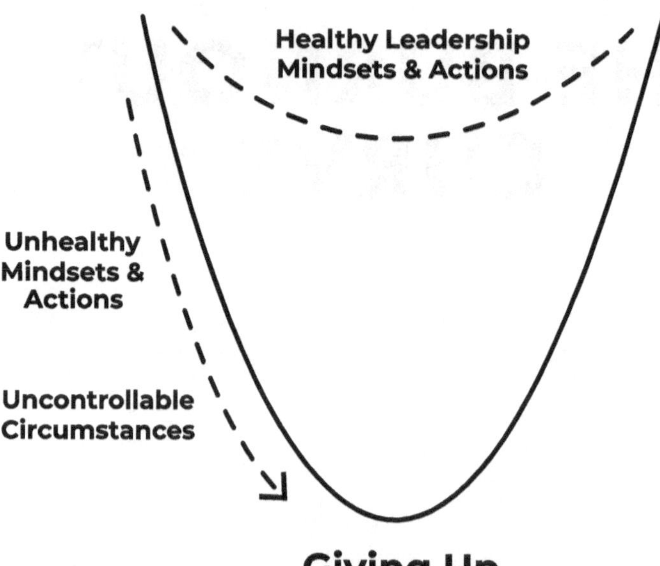

This is the Burnout Curve. Over the years, I developed this visual construct as a way to illustrate how burnout works. But don't let that deep smile of a curve fool you. The Burnout Curve is not a happy place to exist, and we are all susceptible to its gravitational pull every moment of every day.

Sustainable Impact

In the upper-right corner of The Burnout Curve, you see our target, Sustainable Impact. Sustainable Impact is the outcome we are after in every area of our lives — in our personal growth, in our family life, and in our work. Here's how we define it:

———

Sustainable Impact is the multiplied impact of living your purpose with patience and healthy rhythms.

———

Burnout knows that if we are able to get up each day and successfully live out our purpose, we will have a positive impact. That impact will make the world undeniably better for someone, sometimes in grand fashion, but more often in small ways. Burnout despises us and our potential impact. It knows that purpose and impact are fuel that can help propel us to escape The Burnout Curve. More than anything, burnout wants to keep us distracted and chasing false measures of success. It wants us focused on ego and appearance rather than reality. The more we are chasing the appearance of success rather than our true purpose, the more likely we are to remain trapped in burnout.

At this point in our journey, true success will be defined by whether or not we can operate with Sustainable Impact each day. If success is normally about an endpoint, Sustainable Impact is about a rhythm. When we are in that rhythm, we and our team finish each day tired but fulfilled. We work incredibly hard to have the impact we have, and when we recognize the impact, it provides us energy to keep moving forward, and a reminder that we matter. Combine that with the throttle of healthy rhythms and patience, and we have a recipe to continue this journey as long as we want, never being forced so deep into The Burnout Curve that we give up.

As we chase our purpose sustainably, there is a multiplication effect that begins to take hold. The positive impact we have becomes larger than we could have ever imagined. However, that multiplication only happens with the regular practice of patience and healthy rhythms. Operating consistently with Sustainable Impact creates a new version of us; it unlocks our full potential for leadership and impact.

I have been operating with Sustainable Impact for a few years now. My team is also achieving this goal together. It's an incredible way of being because it preserves all the capacity we have to align with our purpose, do our most sacred work, and enjoy life. It is the true opposite of burnout. I have noticed that when I'm intentional about creating Sustainable Impact, I'm able to find joy every day. I very clearly see the positive impact we have on people's lives. I'm driven — beyond what I ever thought possible — to continue this journey.

If you've ever thought that people who love Mondays are insane, you've probably never experienced Sustainable Impact. It is the Holy Grail of being. It means we are holding steady at our best *and* we are truly of service to others.

The Beginning

Creating Sustainable Impact requires practice and discipline. No matter how well we created it yesterday, we still start each new day in the same place: the beginning. In many ways, we are wired for the beginning of things. Beginnings are about possibility and hope. Each new day can be a new opportunity.

We are designed to love the beginning. From new jobs to new relationships, there is something special about the beginning. This period is where our brain is constantly making new discoveries, and each time it does, it gets that hit of dopamine we discussed earlier.

The best example of this is the beginning of a romantic relationship. I've been married for almost twenty-five years. I can tell you, my relationship with my wife now feels *nothing* like it felt in the first year. This is true for all of us because the beginning of a relationship is *weird*. It's like we're experiencing everything with heightened senses. Every look, gesture, and touch has added meaning and an electric charge.

In the beginning, every new thing we learn about a person is a discovery. We spend weeks *soaking* in dopamine. And it isn't the usual drip-feed so much as a deep ocean of crashing waves. We sit across from them on a date as they cut their steak. *Look at the way they chew; it's so cute,* we think, our brain dousing us in good feelings.

Fast forward one year. *If the person across from me does not stop chewing — that wretched, mind-bending, nails-on-a-chalkboard chewing — I am going to lose it.*

Dopamine, like the beginning of things, does not last. As the chemical fades, the challenges become apparent. That new relationship (or job!) is going to be more difficult than we expected. With this realization, the challenges can begin to pummel us. This is where we start to slide down The Burnout Curve.

The Gravity of The Burnout Curve

The sides of The Burnout Curve are steep, and the gravity is intense. Falling into The Burnout Curve happens because of two factors: The first factor involves our own unhealthy mindsets and actions. Our choices determine the version of us that shows up to lead, and as humans, we create more of what we already are. If we show up as a healthy leader, we will create growth and life all around us. If we show up as unhealthy, we will drain life with every reaction or interaction. In a later chapter, we'll look at how we stay trapped in cycles of unhealthy mindsets and actions. Choosing unhealthy mindsets and actions can be as simple as working too many hours, as commonplace as believing it is a weakness to ask for help, or as serious as leaving trauma unresolved.

This leads into the second factor that makes us susceptible to The Burnout Curve: uncontrollable circumstances. For many of us, uncontrollable circumstances make up our entire day. We will inevitably face challenges that are completely outside of our control. When this happens, all the choices we've made and all the mindsets we've cultivated, whether healthy or not, will determine how well we can respond. If our daily rhythms are made up of unhealthy habits, our response to the initial challenges will be equally unhealthy.

You wake up energized for the day. Your plan is to invest in yourself this morning and then tackle some big tasks. *It's going to be such a productive day.* Then you reach over to the nightstand and grab your phone. Muscle memory causes you to tap your email app. There, in your inbox, sits *Carl* already dropping little bombs guaranteed to blow up your day. You dive straight into the stress. Twelve hours later, you sit amongst the debris of your original plan for the day. *Did I even do anything?* Sure, you spent your entire day putting out fires (many set by that little arsonist, *Carl*), but you checked off exactly zero of the most important tasks you had planned for.

As dopamine wears off and the first challenges begin to hit, we can fall headfirst into The Burnout Curve. Gravity takes over, pulling us down faster and faster. Once gravity is in charge, the problems seem to come in quick succession. Before we know it, our days seem to consist entirely of moving from issue to issue, our exhaustion increasingly dictating our responses. Our frustration grows, leading to anger and discontent.

This is a picture of what *many* of our days can look like. The uncontrollable circumstances will always be there. The question will be, how do we respond? Are we showing up in a way that allows us to respond positively?

Get To vs. Have To

Inevitably, my best days are ones where I look around and think, *Can you believe I get to do this?* There is excitement when we *get* to do something. It's not about the thing being new, it's about the privilege and blessing of being able to do it. And when we get paid to do it, that's even better! But as we slide deeper into The Burnout Curve, our mindset will shift from "I *get* to do this" to "I *have* to do this."

"Get to" is one of the first things that burnout destroys. It knows that when we "have to," everything becomes a burden instead of a blessing. We are no longer focused on how we're impacting others with the work we "get to" do. Instead, we're focused on how things negatively affect us because we "have to" do them. When we are healthy leaders, we are outwardly focused, serving others. The more we burn out, the more we become inwardly focused, wanting to know why others aren't serving us.

When my kids were young, and I was wildly burned out, I didn't get to be a parent. I had to be a parent. When my team and I were burned out, we didn't get to work with our clients. We had to.

Jennifer Moss has a great take on this concept: "If you perform a work-related action because you have to, that is defined as movement, but if you perform a work-related action because you want to, that is defined as motivation."[1]

The further we dip into burnout, the more we lose motivation. Then our movement (and our service to others) is not coming from a well of energy and excitement. Instead, burnout drains our very limited resources, like someone has upended our cup and it is rapidly spilling out.

Giving Up

We can only spend so long operating in "have to" mode before our cup is completely empty and we hit the bottom of The Burnout Curve. The bottom of The Curve is not a place of brightness and warmth. It is a place of hopelessness and isolation. At the bottom of The Burnout Curve, the four major signs of burnout we discussed — overwhelm, fatigue, cynicism, and loneliness —

now rule. Like the Four Horsemen of the Apocalypse, these signs dominate our thinking and signal an upcoming breaking point. The only question is, how large will the breaking point be?

The breaking point can be as simple as saying or thinking, "I give up." Maybe it's getting out of a relationship, quitting a job, or taking a demotion. The longer we remain at the bottom of The Burnout Curve, the more likely we are to give in to negative coping mechanisms, like alcohol or substance abuse. The results can be as dark as giving up on our teams or families, or even ending our own lives.

A note on giving up: There are times that we *need* to give up on a situation. We should not stay in abusive relationships, with cruel bosses, or in oppressive organizations. Exiting these situations is a good form of giving up. The negative form of giving up is leaving or quitting something that is potentially *very good*. At the bottom of The Burnout Curve, we don't have the capacity to continue fighting for that potential good.

If you look at The Burnout Curve illustration and can identify yourself as being at the bottom of The Curve, then you do not have to wait until you finish this book to get help. At the bottom, you *will* need others to help you find your way out. I needed The Back Porch Intervention.

We are all susceptible to The Burnout Curve, and it's easy to get trapped at the bottom. As we go through the book, we're going to dive into why we remain trapped and how to reclaim the elements that keep us trapped. This will enable us to make better choices for ourselves. One of those better choices will be *reaching out to others* for help. Feel free to skip to that step now and reach out for the help you need — whether it's from a trusted friend or a professional therapist. *Do not sit at the bottom of The Burnout Curve alone!*

Making The Curve Shallow

If showing up with unhealthy mindsets and taking unhealthy actions are what make us susceptible to falling deep into The Burnout Curve, then our number-one job each day is to show up with healthy mindsets and take healthy actions. This serves to make The Burnout Curve as shallow as it can be. Then, when uncontrollable circumstances hit us and we get knocked into The Burnout Curve, it's shallow enough that we can step right out again, getting back to Sustainable Impact.

This year, my family and I experienced some challenges that would have historically gone very badly for everyone. When the stress of the challenges showed up, if I had existed deep in The Burnout Curve like I used to, I would have responded in a terrible way. I would have been deeply upset, and I would have made sure everyone around me was deeply upset as well. Instead, I noticed that while the stress knocked me into The Curve, The Curve was very shallow. That's because I now do the work every day to make it that way. I was able to step back into Sustainable Impact with relative ease. I was able to lead my family in a way that created stability and hope. It just took a regular practice of ensuring I invested in myself to show up as a healthy leader.

Sounds simple, right? Just show up with a healthy mindset and take healthy action. So why do we keep finding ourselves sitting at the bottom of The Burnout Curve wondering if we'll ever get out? In Part 2: The Anatomy of a Trap, I'll talk about why we make choices that keep us trapped at the bottom, racing toward breaking points where we might give up.

CHAPTER 3 REFLECTION

Reflection Questions

1. Describe a time when your own unhealthy mindsets or actions caused you to react to a situation in an unhealthy way. How do you wish you had reacted differently?

2. Describe a situation when you can clearly remember going from a "get to" mindset to a "have to" mindset. Were you able to switch back to "get to" in that situation?

3. Describe a time when you felt so burned out (and probably alone) that you chose to give up on something that was potentially very good.

....

....

....

....

....

....

....

Take Action

Write down choices you make that bring life back to you. This simple list will help you get back on track if you ever notice yourself getting into "have to" mode. What are those healthy choices you know you can make that give you the capacity to continue the journey?

CHAPTER 3 ENDNOTES

1. Jennifer Moss, *The Burnout Epidemic: The Rise of Chronic Stress and How We Can Fix It* (Harvard Business Review Press, 2021), 19.

Part 2

ANATOMY OF A TRAP

"A trap is only
a trap if you don't
know about it.
If you know
about it,
it's a challenge."

— China Miéville,
King Rat

Chapter 4

THE BOULDER

Early in life, we are taught to take on responsibility and live up to whatever that responsibility asks of us. In a broad sense, we can see this as a definition of success. Learning to make commitments and fulfill them is one of the primary lessons of childhood. At some point, we are given responsibility for using the bathroom on our own. Those first few months are often rocky in that regard, but eventually we start to figure it out. As we do, we are praised for our success. "Way to go, buddy; you pooped in the potty!"

Along that path of growth, we learn that fulfilling responsibilities leads to praise and rewards. We progress from using the bathroom on our own, to riding a bike, to turning in homework, to checking off our Q2 goals. Along that journey, we go from being praised for using the potty (at a certain age, someone cheering for you while you go is just *awkward*), to receiving promotions and bonuses for our work. The relationship between fulfilling responsibility and praise can cause us to take on more and more. Eventually that weight becomes a heavy burden.

This can be easily visualized as a person pushing a boulder up a mountain because that is how it feels most days. That boulder is made up of all the commitments. While we are taught to make and keep commitments, we are rarely taught how to judge *if* we should take something on in the first place. Opportunity is knocking, after all. It would be *rude* not to answer. Because we don't have a strong filter to determine if we should take something on, we default to yes. We are conditioned early on by reward to say yes, and shamed if we say no.

Which brings us to the boulder. The image of a man or woman pushing a boulder up a mountain has become an almost universal image to represent success. If living up to responsibilities is a basic definition of success, and those commitments make up our boulder, then the image of the boulder being pushed by one person is the visual representation of our value. It would stand to reason, then, that the larger the boulder, the more valuable we are. Which brings us to the next component of the boulder analogy — lies.

Liar, Liar, Pants on Fire

Go back to the idea that society is a success-generating machine that uses us as fuel. What the machine has learned is that if we believe certain things about the boulder, then we will run farther and faster, thereby generating more success. The fact that the things it asks us to believe are *lies* is irrelevant to the machine. As is the fact that the people pushing the boulder up the mountain eventually break when the weight becomes too great. Human beings, it turns out, are a great renewable resource. When one falls, they are simply replaced with the next one in line.

I want you to hear something very important: *Breaking this cycle of burnout does not mean we have to break the entire machine.* We can find meaningful impact and success even as we win the daily battle with burnout. *Both are possible.* Many people assume that defeating burnout simply means working less. They believe less burnout equals less productivity, which will lead to less success. I would argue that when we show up rested, focused, driven, patient, and optimistic, we are going to get *more important* work done. We are going to lead our teams in a way that creates steadiness and excitement, enabling more success, not less.

However, if we want to introduce any sustainability to the machine, we have to first understand the lies about pushing the boulder that we have come to believe as truths.

Lie #1: *The larger our boulder, the stronger and more successful we are.*

Because we are rewarded for making and living up to commitments, we naturally default to thinking *bigger is better*. More commitments mean more praise. The size of our boulder becomes a demonstration to the outside world that we are "successful." We often see this in the most common conversation:

"Hey, how are you doing?"

"Oh man, I'm *so* busy."

That simple two-line exchange is a verbal representation of the size of a boulder. Busyness demonstrates how important we are. So much of our value and identity is tied up in the boulder because we have fully bought into the lie that the larger the boulder, the stronger and more "successful" we are. So we commit, and often overcommit. When "bigger" and "more" are the drivers for our lives, we will eventually add so much weight to the boulder — so many commitments — that we can no longer hold it up.

The truth is that most of our boulders are made of unintentional choices that look good from the outside, but should never have been made in the first place. Most of us are not pushing the boulder up the mountain; rather, we are often struggling just to keep it from rolling back over and wrecking everything.

As I sat through The Back Porch Intervention, the weight of my boulder was so great, I was completely unable to make progress up the mountain. I had made so many commitments — each in service of an image that I was doing well — that I could not hope to fulfill them all. And yet, if you'd asked me how I was doing at the time, I probably would have pointed to the size of my boulder with pride and said, "Oh man, I'm *so* busy."

Lie #2: Strength is having the sheer force of will to push the boulder up the mountain alone.

So many of our challenges as a society go back to our misguided definitions of strength and weakness. We are taught over and over that needing others is weakness and accomplishing things alone is proof of our strength. This leads to a tremendous amount of isolation and loneliness. There are days when we absolutely cannot support the weight of our commitments, but asking for help would demonstrate weakness, so we sit quietly, straining under the weight of our choices.

If we end up at the bottom of The Burnout Curve sitting underneath our boulder, unwilling to ask for help, we will never be able to get out. *Escaping the depths of The Burnout Curve requires other people*. We will not find the help we need by remaining silent.

The strong, silent type is the archetypal hero who always wins in the end. Unfortunately, it's an unattainable (and, frankly, fictitious) ideal. Even as you read this, there is probably a part of you saying, "No, I'm really good on my own. I don't need others." Maybe. If so, God bless. I'm glad it works for you. It might also mean you haven't yet hit a breaking point large enough to force you to ask for help. If (or when) that breaking point comes, the only way through it is to embrace the truth that we need each other. And the fastest way to find support is by mustering the *strength* to say three magical words: I need help.

Lie #3: The mountain has a top and when we reach it, we can put our boulder down.

When we take on a commitment and add it to our boulder, we justify it by thinking we won't have to push it forever. There will be a point where we can put the weight down. That point is the top of the mountain. Eventually, we will push our boulder so far up the mountain that it will reach the top and roll right over the other side. We'll be free of the burden we have labored under for so long.

Often, that is the picture of retirement. If we simply reach a certain level of success or live long enough, we can put it all down and relax. The problem is, there is no top to this mountain. It is what author James P. Carse calls an "infinite game."[1] Simon Sinek popularized the idea in his 2019 book, *The Infinite Game.*[2] In an infinite game, the entire goal is to stay in the game. There is no end point. Just stay in the game.

Unfortunately, if you look at how we are living our lives — pushing the boulder up the mountain — it's clear we believe there is a point where we will declare victory. Even if we do make it to the point of retirement, we will still have six or seven decades of muscle memory that caused us to add to the size of our boulder. To think we'll be able to suddenly choose a different way of making choices is laughable.

Instead, if we believed we were playing an infinite game, we would make far more sustainable choices. Knowing the goal is to stay in the game, not to win it, we would undoubtedly reprioritize our time and establish healthy boundaries and rhythms. We would be able to prioritize our own health and growth, guilt free, because that would lead to longevity and ongoing impact.

Lie #4: Everyone else is pushing their boulder up the mountain just fine.

As we sit under our boulder, worried that we can't actually support it, we look around and see everyone else whistling happily while they push their boulders up the mountain. We believe this is true because we see evidence of it through brief glimpses into their lives. Conversations, meetings, or social media all become narrow windows into their perfect lives. What we fail to take into account is the *curation* that dictates exactly what we see in those brief glimpses.

Because everyone around us was also taught that pushing a massive boulder up the mountain alone is strength, they carefully curate everyone's view of their lives. Each time you meet them and ask how they are doing, their answers are calculated to present the best picture possible. Every time they post on social media, their words and images are carefully chosen to help everyone else understand that they have it all together. This isn't everyone all the time, but I'm comfortable saying it's most of us, most of the time.

What we don't see in these fleeting looks at their lives is the rest of the picture. It's easy to make the other side of the window look beautiful. For most of us, the rest of the house is a disaster. No one sees the quiet moments where we worry about our lives. No one sees us at 3:00 a.m., struggling to sleep because stress dominates us and we can't get our brains to shut off. No one sees our anxiety about money, business, and family. No one sees *the truth*. The truth is, life is hard and we are all doing the best we can. The truth is, no one is successfully pushing the boulder up the mountain — not consistently, and certainly not alone.

Belief in these collective lies about the boulder generates overcommitment and isolation. The size of the boulder increases and our resilience decreases. It also generates two distinct emotions: fear and shame.

Fear and Shame

If burnout is the general leading the war against us, fear and shame are its lieutenants. Each day, they conspire to execute burnout's battleplan. They are the emotions that ensure we remain trapped in The Burnout Curve.

Under the shadow of the boulder, fear is our constant companion. And, let's be honest, fear is a crappy roommate. Fear tells us how everything will go wrong while also ensuring we are unable to see possibility, to find or hold onto *hope*. Fear sits beside us at work, reminding us of all the terrible possibilities that exist. It snuggles up beside us in bed each night, whispering terror into our ears.

Shame is the emotion that tells us we should listen to our fear. Why? Because we are broken. We are helpless. We are frauds. We are imposters. We are liars. We are fake. We are weak. We are inadequate. We are worthless. We are unloveable.

We are not enough.

Shame holds the tip of its thumb and forefinger together and says, "All those things are true, and everyone is *this* close to figuring it out."

Fear startles us by chiming in over our shoulder, "And when they figure it out, all of this will come crashing down." Fear begins to dominate our decision-making process. Fear of judgment. Fear of loss. Fear of pain. Fear of being found out.

We spend so much time listening to the insidious duet sung by fear and shame that we believe what they say. We begin to believe that we are broken and this will all come crashing down. We hide from this story under our boulders, praying that no one will ever see that truth. This is why we continue to overcommit in order to increase the size of the boulder. The larger the boulder, the easier it is to hide under its perceived meaning.

The problem is that fear and shame are lying to us. Fear was intended to keep us safe. Back when sabretooth tigers were prowling our neighborhoods on a regular basis, fear was very helpful. There are still times when fear is actually helpful. When we are young or in a dangerous situation, fear can keep us from harm. The fear instilled in me as a child kept me safe — *when I was a child*. However, if that same fear is still making choices for me as a forty-five-year-old man, it is no longer helpful. Rather than keeping us safe, fear and shame keep us small and contained — trapped under the boulder.

Loneliness and Vulnerability

One of the ways fear and shame keep us trapped is by preventing us from asking for help. We are convinced that whoever we ask will see our weakness and judge us, generating even *more* shame. Because we cannot be vulnerable with anyone around us, it leads to deep loneliness. We sit alone under the weight of the boulder, aware that we can't hold it up forever but unable to see a way out. The irony of all this is that the lies we believe about the boulder, combined with fear and shame, rob us of the very thing that would allow us to escape The Burnout Curve — help from others.

Healthy vulnerability is one of the keys to great leadership, and it's even more important when we are leading ourselves. As I've noted, our ability to open up and admit that we need help *solves* loneliness. In almost every case where we admit our needs, people rush in to serve us. We find out, in that moment, that we are *not* alone. When we ask for help and are served by people who care about us, we can find peace. In that peace, we can begin to recognize that the stories fear and shame are telling us are lies.

Yes and No

Ultimately, our belief in the significance of a large boulder combined with our fear and shame drive us to say yes repeatedly. This just adds to the size of the already unsustainable boulder. Saying no is associated with weakness, so we default to yes, and only use no when we are forced to by a breaking point. Eventually, the path to health involves learning to say no intentionally, rather than requiring a breaking point. This means, we have to learn to rewrite the stories fear and shame tell us. We must recognize their stories as the lies they are, and replace them with stories that empower us to make intentional choices. In later chapters, we will dive into how to recognize disempowered stories and learn how to rewrite them.

Eventually, being able to chip away at the weight we carry will involve being far more intentional about our commitments. When we make choices based on the stories fear and shame tell us, we are actually running on a type of autopilot rather than being intentional. These emotions and stories dictate that we simply say yes to every opportunity. This frees us from having to think critically about how a commitment or expectation we're about to take on really fits into our life. It frees us from even needing a plan for our lives. (Simply run from yes to yes to yes, and eventually it will all work out, right?) It frees us from having challenging conversations by saying no. It frees us from the fear of possibly disappointing others.

It also doesn't help that the yes is so attractive. When we say yes, it can sometimes be driven by seemingly good things, like pride, value, and service. There is a high that comes with being asked to do something — perhaps it's even an honor — so we default to the yes in order to prove our value.

Unfortunately, all those yeses add up to the unsustainable weight of our boulder. As it stands, we default to yes, and it takes an Act of Congress to get us to change our minds to no, to admit that we can't (or even don't want to) do something. A more sustainable path could involve defaulting to no — unless the opportunity lines up with our goals, capabilities, and most importantly, our *capacity*.

The boulder concept is hard to wrestle with because we are taking most of what we have been taught throughout our lives about success and strength, and turning it upside down. That process is difficult because we have so much muscle memory built up. Even though I understand that the boulder is a trap, and I know how to escape the trap, I still find myself occasionally defaulting back to the old ways — overcommitting and hiding under the boulder, pretending I have my life together.

Learning to live our lives unleashed from the trap of the boulder means we have to intentionally *create* our lives. We have to choose a vision for our future, who we need to be to create that reality, and then take action. This will require intentionality at every step. Creating a sustainable life encompasses everything from big plans to moment-to-moment choices. We will no longer give over our lives to fear and shame, forfeiting our future to burnout and eventual ruin.

We are in charge.

I fully acknowledge that the previous chapters are hard to row through because they are about the problem. And exploring the problem, in this case, can be deeply disturbing because it causes us to question much of what we have built our lives on. Unfortunately, we need to fully understand the problem before we can find the solution. But rest assured, the solution is coming. We're in this together.

CHAPTER 4 REFLECTION

Reflection Questions

1. What lies about the boulder have you believed?

2. Describe a time when fear or shame stopped you from doing something you *knew* you should do.

3. Describe a situation in which you said yes to something even
    though you *knew* you didn't have the capacity to take the
    thing on. What did that situation cost you?

....

....

....

....

....

....

Take Action

Think about your life and the role the boulder plays. Write down
everything you can think of that makes up your boulder. What
weight are you attempting to push up the mountain? Identify any
prior commitments that you need to put down.

CHAPTER 4 ENDNOTES

1.   James P. Carse, *Finite and Infinite Games: A Vision of Life as Play and Possibility* (Free Press, 1986).

2.   Simon Sinek, *The Infinite Game* (Penguin Random House, 2019).

"The greatest trap in our life is not success, popularity or power, but self-rejection."

— Henri Nouwen,
priest

Chapter 5

THE THREE ELEMENTS THAT KEEP YOU TRAPPED

THE BURNOUT CYCLE

Now that we understand our enemy — burnout — and our relationship to the boulder, we need to understand the three elements that will keep us trapped under the weight of our lives. These three elements combine to create a perpetual cycle that increases the size of the boulder we are attempting to shove up the mountain. The cycle also decreases our capacity to invest in our own health and ensures burnout will dominate our lives.

In the introduction, I told you that I decided to write this book to answer one question: Why do smart people refuse to do the simple things needed to win the battle against burnout? In search of the answer, we began by deploying a survey to understand why people choose not to rest when they have the opportunity. I was genuinely surprised where the results led us. The majority of the answers contained three themes that shaped the course of this work — identity, expectations, and judgment.

In this chapter, we'll briefly look at each of these elements and the cycles they create. In future chapters, we'll do a deep dive into each element.

Identity

There are two questions that shape the course of our lives: "Who am I?" and "Do I matter?" The first is a question of identity, and the second a question of purpose. The questions are so intertwined, it can be difficult to understand if our identity defines our purpose or the other way around. For the purposes of this book, we'll think of identity as who we are meant to be, and our purpose as the way we are meant to impact the world.

What we believe about our identity is often twisted very early in life by outside forces. Shame, circumstance, and family history shape our view of who we are at our core. These forces can combine to tell us a lie: "You are broken. You are not enough." The future we create is based on our identity, and an identity of brokenness will create a future of perpetual burnout.

Psychiatrist, physician, and spiritual teacher Sir David Hawkins said, "The unconscious will allow us to have only what we think we deserve. The more we hang on to our negativity and the small self-image that results, the less we think we deserve, and we unconsciously deny ourselves the abundance which flows so easily to others…. If we have a small view of ourselves, then what we deserve is poverty, and our unconscious will see to it that we have that actuality."[1]

Rather than creating a life of impact based on the truth that we are enough and have nothing to prove, we embrace the idea that we are fundamentally broken. The life created with that story as the driver is one of neverending struggle to prove that we are okay.

You might be saying, "I don't think I'm broken." That would be great, but in my experience, you would be the outlier, not the norm. Belief that we are not enough often manifests as decisions that are meant to prove something, either to ourselves or to others. Think through your life and the number of choices you made with the core purpose of proving something. How often have you made a big purchase, taken on a task, or not taken action for yourself in order to prove something?

Early in our marriage we bought a brand-new 2001 Dodge Durango that we could not afford. For my part of the purchase decision, it was genuinely to show everyone around me that I was doing great. It didn't take long before the financial burden began weighing on us and causing a tremendous amount of stress. I distinctly remember one clear moment where I *knew* the right thing to do was to sell it and get something we could afford. I couldn't bring myself to do it, however. *What would that say about me?* The situation started with a need to prove something because my identity was one of brokenness. The situation was perpetuated because I had to maintain the illusion that everything was great. We endured stress and turmoil that should have never entered our home. I let it in because of an identity crisis that was causing me to need to prove myself.

When we operate from an identity of brokenness, we frequently take on the second element: unsustainable expectations.

Unsustainable Expectations

In an effort to prove that we are okay, we take on expectations. These expectations are often presented to us by society, our families, jobs, or even our fear.

"If I become a doctor, I'll prove to my parents that I'm enough."

"If I work through my vacation, I'll prove to my boss that I'm enough."

Whether we actually *want* to be a doctor (maybe) or work through our vacation (never) doesn't weigh as heavily in our decision-making process as the expectations. These expectations are given to us, but ultimately we have to decide if we are going to live our lives with them in place. When we accept them, we use them as the new bar for success that we must clear.

An expectation taken on in order to prove something about ourselves will often become unsustainable. Here's how I define unsustainable expectations:

———

Expectations that are unreasonable, unattainable, unhealthy, or unwanted.

———

Unsustainable expectations contribute to a cycle of burnout and an eventual breaking point. In Chapter 7, we will explore each part of this definition to discover what really makes these expectations unsustainable. You might also be asking yourself, "Well, what does a *sustainable* expectation look like?" An expectation only becomes sustainable when it is achievable, aligns with our vision for our lives, contributes to our impact, isn't chosen to prove anything, and doesn't exceed our capacity.

In the case of the infamous Dodge Durango, I can identify a few different unsustainable expectations that were driving me. For starters, I had taken on the societal expectation of what a "successful" person does (they buy shiny cars).

I had been told for years that I was advanced for my age. It was time to prove it. This became an expectation that I do things early in life. None of my friends at that age had families or were driving cars that nice. (Yes, in 2001, for us, a Dodge Durango was nice. I'll hear no blasphemy of that vehicle.)

I had even turned the example of my father into an internal

expectation of what a successful husband and father does — he quietly provides through hard work with no drama. Returning a *major* purchase would be *major* drama, as well as proof I was struggling to provide for my family.

There are probably even more expectations involved in this situation, but those three alone were enough to cause me to make decisions that were counter to what would have been best for us.

We feel like we are not enough, so we take on unsustainable expectations to try to prove that we are enough. When we struggle to achieve those expectations, we then experience the third element that keeps us trapped: judgment.

Judgment

Using the expectations we have taken on as a framework for determining success or failure, we then judge ourselves. We compare every result to this ideal, and often find ourselves lacking.

Did we live up to the expectation? Did we fail to live up to the expectation? Did we eventually live up to the expectation but struggle to do so? Did we lie, cheat, or steal to live up to the expectation?

We judge ourselves based on the expectations we have taken on, but we also have to remember that how we judge ourselves is not based on objective truth. Back in Chapter 2, we talked about how our brain is designed to get a hit of dopamine whenever it finds what it's looking for. This entire cycle began with the *belief* that we are broken. Our brain is looking to confirm that story. How often do we achieve our goal but still feel lacking?

Our mind confirms its belief that we are not enough and receives a hit of dopamine. It feels really good about itself. Unfortunately, the story it confirmed is negative, which then releases cortisol into our system. If dopamine is all about excitement and happiness, cortisol is all about stress and frustration. Like all drug addicts, that high feels good to us for a short time, but then we are left to deal with the toxic aftereffects. The judgment generates fear, stress, and frustration, and we continue living our lives with a seemingly confirmed belief that we are broken.

There is a scene in the 2006 James Bond film *Casino Royale*, where our hero narrowly escapes death in a fight for his life. Afterward, he is staring at himself in the bathroom mirror, trying to wash blood off his body. You can see him reflecting on how he got to that moment and what the life he had chosen was doing to him. That was me, staring in the mirror in 2001, except without the blood, dirt, glorious battle wounds, or Daniel-Craig-level smoldering good looks (but who's counting?). No, it was just me and my fear about my own failures, judging myself incessantly. I knew what I should do with that damned Durango, but I couldn't. The judgment I was enduring internally was extreme. Imagine what the outside world would heap on me if I sold it.

Side note: The idea that *anyone* in the outside world cared what I drove is still laughable, but stop and think how many times we do or don't make a choice because we think others are watching our every move? I was twenty-one at the time, but every once in a while, I can still spot forty-five-year-old me operating with the same mindset.

Using unsustainable expectations as a framework for judgment, we confirm our original thought — we are not enough. This confirmation leads us straight back to identity, creating a loop.

The Burnout Cycle

The weight of our boulder is made up of this self-perpetuating loop: The Burnout Cycle. Operating from an identity of brokenness, we believe we aren't enough, take on unsustainable expectations to prove we are okay, then judge ourselves negatively, proving our original belief. That confirmed belief begins the cycle anew, with more unsustainable expectations, more judgment, and ultimately, more burnout.

With each turn of The Burnout Cycle, our boulder gets bigger and heavier. Eventually, the weight of the expectations we are trying to live up to far outstrips our capacity. For a while, we *are* able to truly push the boulder up the hill. Then we struggle but are still able to maintain appearances to the outside world. Eventually, the weight becomes so great that we are simply trying to keep the boulder from rolling back over and crushing us.

This is survival mode. We aren't meant to be in survival mode for long periods of time, but for many of us, it becomes the norm. We spend every day just trying to make it through that day, only to repeat the same process of just getting by, over and over again. Progress becomes non-existent, our life becomes stagnant, and we fall deeper into The Burnout Curve.

So how did things end with the Durango? Did I have the strength to lay down those unsustainable expectations, sell the vehicle, and set my family on more solid financial ground? Of course, not. I lived with the weight of that mid-size family SUV bearing down on my chest for years.

Through the process, the stress, frustration, and fear that were generated caused me to show up as a very unhealthy version of myself. I was quick-tempered and selfish. There was damage done in my marriage and with my oldest son because I was under so much pressure — pressure I had created and sustained.

We endured long enough for me to get a job that paid slightly better and were able to finally afford the vehicle. Of course, I was still operating with the same sense of brokenness and unsustainable expectations. How long do you think it was before we bought an even bigger SUV with the higher payment to match?

And The Burnout Cycle cycled on.

Finding Hope

The three elements — identity, unsustainable expectations, and judgment — keep us trapped at the bottom of The Curve until we eventually lose all capacity to resist. That temptation to give up becomes louder and louder, dominating our thinking. This is the darkness of repeating The Burnout Cycle and staying trapped at the bottom of The Burnout Curve.

However, there is hope. We can reclaim all three of these elements and intentionally use them to go from burnout to momentum. In order to do that, we need to understand each element more deeply. We'll cover them in Chapters 6, 7, and 8. In Chapters 9 and 10, we'll learn a key skill that will give us the ability to reclaim these elements. Then in Chapter 11, we'll learn how to reclaim the three elements and *intentionally build the lives we want.*

CHAPTER 5 REFLECTION

Reflection Questions

1. In what areas of your life are you making decisions to prove that you are enough rather than out of a genuine desire or a sense purpose?

2. What expectations are you currently living under that feel unreasonable, unattainable, unhealthy, or unwanted?

3. When have you judged yourself for failing to live up to an unsustainable expectation?

Take Action

Write a list of unsustainable expectations you have taken on in order to prove something to yourself or someone else. Are you in a position to free yourself from any of those expectations?

CHAPTER 5 ENDNOTES

1.   David R. Hawkins, MD, PhD, *Letting Go: The Pathway of Surrender* (Hay House LLC, 2014), 99.

"To be yourself
in a world that is
constantly trying
to make you
something else
is the greatest
accomplishment."

— Ralph Waldo Emerson

Chapter 6

IDENTITY

Answering the question "Who am I?" is a journey that begins at birth. Even as infants, we are trying to figure out the world, and our place in it. The pursuit of learning who we are is a noble quest. Unfortunately, that quest is often co-opted very early in life and replaced with a different question: "What's wrong with me?"

The Emerson quote on page 92 references "a world that is constantly trying to make you something else." The world shapes us into something other than our authentic selves with a flood of negative messages that all boil down to a core idea — you are not enough. Our early experiences, and the messages we receive, generate shame.

Psychologist Gershen Kaufman wrote, "Shame becomes inevitably bound up with the process of identity formation which underlies man's striving for self, for valuing, and for meaning. The experience of shame is a fundamental sense of being defective as a person, accompanied by fear of exposure and self-protective rage."[1]

These messages of shame come from a variety of sources: our parents, school, friends, peers, coworkers, social media, and advertising. Most loudly, we hear the messages from the voice of shame in our heads.

Perform!

Buy!

Follow the rules!

Shame can generate a wide array of short-term outcomes. It can motivate temporary performance or compliance. However, those positive outcomes will always be coupled with feelings that we are not enough.

Shame puts us at the center of every scenario and shines a light on our perceived brokenness. Our results aren't lacking, *we* are lacking. Our latest quarterly numbers aren't bad, *we* are bad. This often leads to feeling broken, incomplete, or behind.

We need long-term motivation, which is where healthy leadership comes in. In the absence of healthy leadership, we often turn to shame to move the needle. Shame generates short-term outcomes at the cost of long-term damage.

Prove or Punish

When we listen to shame and see ourselves as broken, we then pour our energy into either proving that we aren't broken or punishing ourselves. We then begin living a life that isn't about what we want, but rather what we think will prove that we are okay.

This plays directly into our problem with burnout. How much of our overcommitment is the result of trying to prove something to ourselves or to the outside world? How often do we say yes instead of no in order to prove that we are enough? There will be two key questions we need to ask ourselves to understand if we are operating out of brokenness or completeness.

Do I feel the need to prove anything right now?

Do I feel the need to punish myself for something?

The question about proving things is easier to answer. Think about walking into an important meeting. There might be multiple things we are trying to prove in that room: that we belong, that we deserve a promotion, that we are capable, that we are smart.

When we feel the need to prove something, everything is ultimately about us. We are placing ourselves at the center of the story. This can take seemingly selfless actions and twist them to really be about us. This changes the version of us that shows up to take those actions, and the experience people have of us.

If we show up to serve meals at a soup kitchen in order to prove we are generous, then we aren't actually serving others. We're serving the image that *we* are generous, which is actually selfish. We are putting on the clothes of generosity, but underneath is actually a person who struggles with feelings of inadequacy.

When I am speaking at a conference, if I'm trying to prove that I deserve to be on the stage, then every word I say isn't really about serving the audience. It's about them thinking I'm special, which means there is a man on that stage who questions whether he is enough to be on that stage.

People can feel when we are being self-serving, and it changes their experience of us. Every word is delivered differently and received differently than if I show up aligned with the *truth* — I am enough and have everything it takes to stand on that stage and impact the lives of everyone there. That version of me is capable of *true* service and impact.

Do I feel the need to punish myself for something?

Spotting the desire to punish ourselves for not being enough is harder to see than the need to prove something. Rarely do we sit there and think, "I'm going to punish myself today." However, it will often manifest itself with feelings of being undeserving. We will look at something that would be good for us and not do it because we don't feel like we deserve it.

Again, we go back to how this can contribute to burnout. In our original survey, we asked the question, "When you have the opportunity to rest and choose not to, what is your reasoning?" Many of the answers came down to not having earned the right to rest. We *need* rest, yet we won't take it when we have the chance because we haven't done enough. We are punishing ourselves for our perceived deficiency.

Reflect on the earlier quote from Dr. Hawkins: "If we have a small view of ourselves, then what we deserve is poverty, and our unconscious will see to it that we have that actuality." Feeling the need to punish ourselves for not being enough can have a direct effect on our choices. We will often deny ourselves things that would be good for us because we don't feel we deserve them. On the opposite side, we will do things that are bad for us because our brokenness has earned the punishment.

For almost all of my life, stories I believed about my physical body told me that a long, healthy life was not for me. My body was not enough when compared with others, and that belief about my brokenness led to obvious choices. Why would I bother going to the gym if I was incapable of building muscle like all my peers? Guess where I learned to believe that story. If you said a middle school locker room, you nailed it. I was the short, scrawny nerd with bony arms. Everyone else had veins popping out of their muscled forearms. My brain didn't think, "Bodies develop at different paces." No, it thought, "Your body is broken. And you suck at dodgeball, too." (I have an unscientific theory that 80 percent of all trauma can be traced to school.)

Imagine my shock when I started working with a trainer in late 2019. I walked in and explained that I needed to lose weight but I didn't run because of bad knees.

He gave me a quizzical look and asked, "Why would you *ever* run? Look at your shoulders, man. You're built to lift weights."

I reflected his puzzled look back at him. "I'm sorry, what do you mean I'm meant to lift weights?"

"Have you never lifted weights? Look at your build. You won't be running at my gym. You'll lift. A *lot*."

I walked out of that gym in genuine shock. I realized that even at the age of thirty-nine, the story about myself had not changed since I was in middle school, and my choices reflected it. I had unconsciously punished myself with bad choices because of the story that I wasn't physically enough.

Why would I say no to an entire sleeve of Oreos?

Why would I not treat that large pizza like my own personal pan pizza?

Why would I not have that extra drink, trip to the buffet, or side of ranch?

Despite being six foot two, I had made a lifetime of choices to punish myself because my short, scrawny middle school body didn't measure up to the other boys around me. Damn.

By the Power of Grayskull

Stop and think about the earliest memory of shame that you have. When did you first ask the question, "What's wrong with me?" This question inevitably sets you on a path of trying to prove you are okay, or to punish yourself because it's what you deserve. I can remember the first time I asked that question, and I can see how that moment changed the course of my life.

When I started kindergarten, I had just turned five. At the time, *He-Man and the Masters of the Universe* [2] was the hottest thing on TV for boys my age. A bowl of Fruity Pebbles and watching He-Man fight his sworn enemy, Skeletor, made for an incredible Saturday morning (now that I think about it, that would *still* be an incredible Saturday morning).

When danger would strike, Prince Adam (who was He-Man's secret identity) would raise his sword into the air and speak magical words. "By the Power of Grayskull! I have the power!" Lightning would strike his sword, transforming him into He-Man. *Every boy wanted to be He-Man.* We would spend our weekends running around the house with anything we could find that resembled a sword. It was a good time to be ridding the universe of evil.

Then I went to school on Monday. Even as a new kindergartener, I knew what recess was. I couldn't wait to run out of the school and into the Kingdom of Eternia, to fight the bad guys. As danger loomed over Stanfield Elementary School in Snyder, Texas, I knew the only way to save the day was to become He-Man. Thankfully, I was never without my imaginary Sword of Power (the administration declined to let me carry an *actual* sword to school). I thrust my pretend blade into the sky and lightning struck, transforming me as I said the words, "By the Power of Grayskull! I have the power." I was no longer Chad Wright, the quiet, blond kid who was half the size of everyone else in the class. I was now He-Man, defender of the universe. And I was sure no one could bully He-Man.

I saw a group of kids across the grassy field already engaged in the battle to save our school. I ran to the crowd, ready to join the fight. As I reached the edge of the group, a boy turned and looked down at me. "What are you doing?" he asked with a sneer.

"I'm He-Man. I'm here to save you," I said earnestly, striking what I assumed was a very heroic pose with my invisible sword held in front of me.

The boy laughed. He closed the distance between us and shoved me in the chest. I flew to the ground, and the impact knocked the wind out of me. Tears immediately sprang to the corners of my eyes as I tried to breathe. My empty lungs screamed at me as he loomed above. I prayed no one would see the tears. Despite my ears ringing and my struggling to breathe, I could still hear his next words, "*You* don't get to play with us."

It turned out, He-Man could be bullied.

I didn't interpret that incident as that kid being a jackass (it would be a few more years before I knew that word). I didn't look at him and see a hurting and misguided six-year-old. No, I looked at that encounter and shame whispered accusingly, "What is wrong with you?"

What is wrong with me?

And so began the quest, not to discover who I was, but to prove that I belonged. Desperately trying to fit in (or at least not stand out), I modified everything I could — to change how people perceived me. I tried to dress and act in a way that matched everyone else. I tried different ways of speaking. I pretended to like things that I actually disliked. In fifth grade, I even tried to change my handwriting. One kid in class had very small, neat handwriting. *No one bullies him. Maybe the handwriting will make a difference.* It didn't. And weirdly enough, my handwriting as an adult is still based on that kid's penmanship.

This quest to prove I belonged shaped my childhood, from elementary to middle to high school. Rarely could I just be myself. In fact, I would be well into my late thirties before I began to really figure out who I was. Shame co-opted decades of my life, causing me to spend my days trying to prove things to others and to punish myself, rather than to show up as my authentic self *in service* to others.

Alignment with Truth

The early experiences that generate shame in our lives keep us focused on the idea that we are broken and need to prove to ourselves (and to the world) that we are enough. The focus on this keeps us out of alignment with the truth, which is that we *are* enough.

You are enough.

I am enough.

We are enough.

We don't need to prove it.

When a baby is born, good parents don't look at him or her and say, "All right, kid, time to prove you deserve our love." That child is enough to have their love simply by *being*. That was true on the first day of your life, and it's still true as you read these words.

The truth is, we are enough and that never changes. What does change is our *alignment* with that truth. When we are aligned with the truth, we operate as our authentic selves. We believe we are enough, so we operate from *being* enough. What does that version of us look like? Answer this question:

Who are you when you are at your best?

Take some time and really think about that. Get out a sheet of paper, the notes app on your phone, or a blank whiteboard. Write down all the words you would use to describe yourself when you are at your best. Now look at it.

That's who you really are.

This is what it is to be complete — to be at your best. You have everything you need today to show up and serve the people around you, impacting their lives for the better.

When we believe we are enough, we are able to shed the external, unsustainable expectations that we've been burdened with. Relieved of the need to prove or punish, we can then make choices that will create the future we want. Alignment with the truth that you are enough allows you to show up as your full self in every situation, providing energy and drive, and increasing the positive impact you have on the world.

Overcoming the Bullshit Response

Early in the process of writing this book, my friend Matthew Wright (no relation, but I do try to convince everyone we're brothers) invited me to present to a group about the ideas I was researching. I spoke about the core ideas of the book. After the event, Matt came up to me and said, "I don't know, man. You are going to have a hard time convincing people that they are enough."

Matt is right. For most of us, we have decades of muscle memory built around the story that we are not enough. We are taught that we are broken, flawed, and failing. In fact, we've spent so long believing in our brokenness, that we see it as truth. When someone says that we are enough, something inside us rebels against that thought. The thought is so foreign that we seek to expel it, like a body ejecting chicken that wasn't cooked long enough.

This is what I call The Bullshit Response. Perhaps your mind is less profane than mine, but the first time someone told me that there was nothing wrong with me, my mind immediately laughed and said, "Bullshit." Try it for yourself.

Sit back in your chair and breathe in deeply.

Say out loud, "I am enough."

It was hard not to laugh, wasn't it? Laugh, cry, snicker, shake your head, or say bullshit. If your initial response to "I am enough" is *anything* other than peace, acceptance, and excitement, then the belief that you are not enough exists somewhere in your being. In Part 3, we'll learn that The Bullshit Response is simply a disempowered story keeping us trapped in burnout, and we'll learn how to unwind that story, creating space for something new.

Unconditional Love

I believe there is a link between believing you are enough and experiencing unconditional love. Unconditional love, like being enough, is an unchangeable state. Unconditional love cannot be earned — that's what makes it unconditional. You also can't do anything to lose it.

On this journey, I've found that accepting that I'm enough has made it easier to accept unconditional love. Or maybe it was accepting unconditional love that made it easier for me to accept that I'm enough. Most likely, it was a little of both.

Many people struggle with the idea of unconditional love. It's often difficult to even believe it exists, or that we might be worthy of it. I've spent my life as a practicing Christian. Even in our circles, where we believe in, and preach, unconditional love, we struggle to truly accept it. We default to the belief that unconditional love exists, but not really for us. We sometimes believe we are the outlier, so bad that we are unworthy of the thing that cannot be earned or lost. Yeah, it makes no sense, but this is how strong the belief in our brokenness is.

Parents can be an example of unconditional love. My parents love my brother and me with no qualification. There is no asterisk next to their love with an attached disclaimer about all the things I could do to lose that love. I could call my parents with any news, good or bad, and they would love me no less after the call than before.

In the same way, enough is a state of being that doesn't change. You can never be more enough or less enough. Each day, you are enough. Can you learn something new today that will increase your capacity to do more good tomorrow? Absolutely. But that doesn't mean you are more enough tomorrow or less enough today.

Enough is enough, and unconditional love is unconditional.

Answer the following question:

How do you experience unconditional love?

People experience unconditional love in many different ways. Some experience it through their faith practices and belief in a higher power, and some through their parents and family. Others have those ride-or-die friends who would follow them to prison. Unconditional love, at its most fundamental level, can always be experienced by getting a dog. No matter what happens, that dog will always be excited to see you simply because you are *you.*

Our dog, London, is a five-pound Teacup Yorkie. Every bit of that five pounds is fur, fury, and love — she believes she is closer to Wookie-size than Yorkie-size. It doesn't matter if I've been gone for six hours or six days, she meets me at the door with the same energy, and will not leave me alone until I pick her up and rest her against my chest. There, she proceeds to snuggle her little head up under my beard. That dog loves me unconditionally. I don't need to prove anything to her, I simply need to *be*.

And for all you cat people out there, please don't come at me about not using them as an example. You know their love is *very* conditional.

Our Identity and Our Work

We often try to shore up our seemingly broken identities through our work. It can become difficult to tell where the work ends and the person begins. For many, their work *is* their identity.

This is seen commonly in law enforcement. When they start as fresh recruits, officers are all taught to make sure policing doesn't become their entire identity. Despite that warning, they will slowly whittle down their friend group until it only contains fellow officers. Their off hours are often eaten up with "off-duty" assignments to earn extra money. This means the vast majority of their hours are dedicated to the job in one way or the other. Over the course of a thirty-year career, their job becomes their entire identity. Eventually, they give their final "10-7" radio call and retire. Overnight, everything that makes up their identity is ripped away. They watch as the department, city, and world moves on without them.

It might be easy to look at that example and shake your head in pity. But take the words "law enforcement" and "police officer" out of those sentences. Replace them with your field of work and title. I'm guessing those sentences still apply to you — because you are susceptible to the trap of turning your work into your identity, too.

Fear vs. Hope

The belief that we are "not enough" is rooted in fear. Anxiety about measuring up means we are always looking for proof that we are right about being broken. This creates a fear-driven operating system that we use to experience the world. Fear finds plenty of reasons why things won't work. This belief that we are lacking will prevent us from taking risks, experimenting, or taking a good, old-fashioned leap of faith.

Embracing the truth that we are enough breeds hope. When we are freed of the burden of needing to prove things, we can then do the work of intentionally creating the life we want. As I have progressed down this road of accepting who I am, I have become far more hope-driven than fear-driven. Why? Because I have learned that when I operate from the truth of being enough, I am capable of creating an incredibly exciting reality for myself and those around me.

Over the next week, I want you to think about this question:

What would I do if I had nothing to prove?

Write down any thoughts you have. Think about the life you could create if you were free of that burden. I know that many of the participants in our survey would instantly get more rest. In response to questions about why they didn't rest, many of their answers boiled down to needing to prove something. Free of that, they could take their nights, weekends, and vacations, and intentionally use them to create a better life for themselves. A well-rested version of all of us will experience life very differently. Well-rested, we also have more capacity for positive impact.

What else would you do? Would you take a leap into a new industry, finally apply for a better job, or ask out that person you've been too nervous to talk to? Would you start your own business, adopt a child, or finally write that book? (Side note: Writing a book is really hard work, but *totally* worth it.)

What would your life look like if you consistently showed up as your best self — with nothing to prove?

Finding Peace and Rest

There is a profound peace to be found when we are operating from a place of wholeness. If we are enough, then by extension, our efforts are enough. Does that mean our efforts are always enough to accomplish every goal we set? Of course not. I feel like I often set a high bar for productivity and then miss it. However, missing that goal doesn't change the fact that I'm still enough, and I should find peace in that truth.

Recently, I was driving home after a hard week. My task list was brimming with unaccomplished items. We'd had a full week serving clients, and I had overestimated how much I could get done between engagements. In the past, shame about those unfinished items would have caused me to drive home and spend another few hours trying to whittle down the list. Why? If I'm honest, it would have been to prove to myself and the people around me that I am a productive, hard working leader.

Free of the need to prove anything, I instead soaked in a peace that I was enough and my efforts were enough. I was then free to answer the question, "What do I *want* to do tonight?" I'm passionate enough about our work that there will be Fridays where I truly *want* to knock a few more items out. However, that night, I *wanted* to pour some Johnnie Walker Blue Label scotch into a glass, sit on my back porch, and reflect with gratitude on an impactful week. And I was *free* to make that choice with no guilt.

Acceptance that we are enough can free us to actually enjoy

life. Our fear is that we will turn into lazy, unproductive, and ultimately, homeless people if we are not constantly driven by anxiety. My experience has been that when I lead with anxiety and fear, I create more problems than I solve. When I lead with peace and hope, I create a better future.

The Burnout Cycle starts with the false belief that we are not enough, and that we either have something to prove or we deserve punishment. Once we begin operating from a place of brokenness, we then take on the second element that keeps us trapped: unsustainable expectations.

CHAPTER 6 REFLECTION

Reflection Questions

1. What early experiences of shame shaped the way you see
    yourself, and how might those experiences still influence your
    choices today?

2. In what situations do you most often feel the need to prove
    something — and how does that affect how you show up for
    others?

3. What would your life look like if you consistently lived in the
    truth that you are enough instead of living in fear or shame?

....

....

....

....

....

....

Take Action

Take ten minutes to write down words and phrases that describe
you when you are at your best. Keep this list somewhere visible
and revisit it daily as a reminder of your authentic identity. This is
who you truly are.

CHAPTER 6 ENDNOTES

1. Gershen Kaufman, "The Meaning of Shame: Toward a Self-Affirming Identity" (Journal of Counseling Psychology, 1974), vol. 21, no. 6, p. 568.

2. *He-Man and the Masters of the Universe* (1983) is a property of Mattel.

"If you accept the expectations of others, especially negative ones, then you will never change the outcome."

— Michael Jordan

Chapter 7

UNSUSTAINABLE EXPECTATIONS

DO MORE!

How do we try to prove that we are enough? This is where expectations come in. Most of our lives are structured around living up to the expectations we choose to accept. Expectations are presented to us from a wide variety of sources. Our first set of expectations often come to us via our parents. We're not long in this world before society begins presenting expectations to us as well. As children, we don't really have a choice to accept or reject expectations. Early in life, we are taught to accept the expectations and then live up to them.

Authors Benjamin Sullivan and Dan Hardy write, "As these children grow up, they're not taught how to determine their own reference point or 'measure of success.' Instead, they adopt the reference points that society deems as 'success' — money, fame, social media likes, etc."[1] When we begin to define expectations for ourselves, we often do it through comparison with others.

I remember falling into a deep depression when I turned twenty-five. Why? Because I had always wanted to write and direct movies, and by the age of twenty-five, Steven Spielberg had directed *Jaws*. That's right. By the age of twenty-five, the greatest director *of all time* had made a film that defined what a summer blockbuster was, causing a massive change in how Hollywood thought about moviemaking. And what had I done? Well, by twenty-five, I had a lovely wife, three sons, and a start-up business. However, none of that measured up because of the (admittedly dumb) expectation I had taken on: that I would have the same impact as Steven Spielberg.

Looking back twenty years, I can see that I was depressed because of one expectation. If I would have shared my concern with *anyone* at the time, they would have helped me see how goofy it was. (Ironically, after writing this section, I reread one of my favorite books, *The Jaws Log* by Carl Gotlieb. It turns out, Steven Spielberg was twenty-seven when he directed *Jaws*. I didn't even have the age correct!)

While we are taught to live up to expectations as a path to success, we rarely discuss the unsustainable nature of accepting every expectation. In Chapter 5, we defined unsustainable expectations:

———

Expectations that are unreasonable, unattainable, unhealthy, or unwanted.

———

Taking on any expectation that is unsustainable will eventually lead to a breaking point. This is because unsustainable expectations use up far more of our capacity. They drain us in ways that contribute to The Burnout Cycle, leaving us lacking the spiritual, emotional, and physical energy needed to thrive.

The "Un" in Unsustainable

Let's look at each aspect of an unsustainable expectation and discover what makes it unsustainable. If an expectation contains any of these qualities, it will ultimately prove to be unsustainable.

Unreasonable - Not guided by or based in good sense

Unreasonable expectations often come to us via comparison. From our earliest days, we are pitted against others to see how we measure up. While this helps us discover how the world is structured, it also teaches us to compare ourselves constantly. Comparison can be helpful if we're intentional with it. Often, however, we compare ourselves with the ideal outlier. The backbone of social media is people presenting a curated view of their lives to make themselves seem like that ideal.

It's not difficult to find female influencers who have babies and immediately jump into reclaiming their bodies — pushing to return to the physical form they had prior to pregnancy. Is that an achievable goal? Sure. Is it reasonable for the majority of women to be expected to return their bodies to their pre-pregnancy state? No. There are a thousand reasons why that's an arduous process for most, and an impossible goal for others.

And yet, if we consume enough content from those influencers, it becomes a temptation to take that unreasonable expectation and measure ourselves against it. This will almost always lead to feelings of being perpetually behind and of not being enough. Comparing ourselves to the outliers is unreasonable.

But if we aim higher, won't we hit higher? Sometimes, sure. But at what cost? Those consistent feelings of being behind, or of not being enough, carry weight. That weight is added to our boulder, and the struggle to push it up the hill becomes that much more difficult. Those unreasonable expectations may feel good to shoot for initially, but we will eventually feel it at the end of a long week, when we just don't have anything left in the tank to try to achieve those goals, and we feel more overwhelmed because of it.

Have you ever found yourself playing the comparison game and taking on unreasonable expectations?

Unattainable - Not able to be reached or achieved

You'd be surprised how often we try to live up to *literally* unattainable expectations. This happens so often because goals cost nothing. They are actually a bit of a trap because we feel good when we set a *huge* goal. I could look at my team tomorrow and say, "We're going to bring in two million dollars in revenue next year." We would start to talk about how great that would be to achieve and all the benefits that would come with it. Setting a massive goal feels exhilarating because we start to think about how good it would feel to achieve that goal.

Setting big goals makes us feel like we *did* something, when in actuality, we just said a large number out loud. And if a large number makes us feel good, why not an even *larger* number? In the tech world, the goal is rarely to create a sustainable business that rewards its employees while improving the lives of its customers for many years to come. No, instead its goal is to be a "unicorn" — a start-up that achieves a valuation of $1,000,000,000. The reason those start-ups are referred to as unicorns is because they are rare enough to be mythical.

Setting goals that are unattainable and chasing them is like trying to outrun the wind. You are probably going to wear yourself out and experience a lot of pain in the process. My coach, Becky Henderson, taught me, "Setting goals is easy. Figuring out who you have to be to achieve them is the hard work."

Have you ever set unattainable expectations and experienced burnout trying to live up to them?

Unhealthy - Harmful to health

If we're trying to create a thriving life in which we routinely win the battle against burnout, *unhealthy* expectations should be the easiest to spot — they will directly and negatively impact our health.

Overwork is one of the biggest side effects of unhealthy expectations. When we accept unhealthy expectations about success and productivity, we will also adopt the unhealthy rhythms that come with them.

When our survey asked why people may choose not to rest, this was one response we received: "I create a strong habit of always being productive with my time, and it's difficult to switch gears into rest mode. With so many pressing issues and needs, it feels indulgent and selfish to take time for myself."

There are a couple of unhealthy expectations in that response. One is the expectation that we must *always* be productive. The other is the expectation that if there are things that need to be done, then rest is *indulgent and selfish*. These two expectations are stories that combine to create a very unhealthy rhythm of constant work and no rest. Since we humans are designed to *need* rest, it's easy to see how this rhythm can decimate our health over a long enough period of time.

Can you spot any unhealthy expectations you have taken? Have they generated burnout or negative health outcomes for you?

Unwanted - Not ever or no longer desired

Unwanted expectations are often external in origin. Friends, family, and society all have very distinct expectations about how we should behave, choices we should make, and goals we should pursue. These expectations aren't all bad, but we don't always do the hard work of sifting through them to intentionally decide which ones we want to agree to. I think we can agree that expecting people to wear shirts and shoes in a restaurant is a *good* expectation. Feeling like you are trapped in your own life because your family *expects* you to become a doctor, lawyer, or (insert your own unwanted career path here), is a very common experience. In this case, the expectation is *unwanted*.

Many expectations come from societal norms. Is it good for a person to complete a college education? That has become the normalized goal in America. In many cases, it can be beneficial, but it is *not* right for everyone. If you are in the latter category and your parents force on you the expectation of earning a college degree, you are going to have four to six years of real struggle and resentment in front of you.

If it is not something we want in the first place, we are going to struggle to consistently live up to it. Unwanted expectations are easy to spot because when we think about them, our faces scrunch up into a scowl.

Can you identify expectations that have been placed on you from an external source that are entirely unwanted?

Race, Gender, and Expectations

This is a good place to talk about societal expectations that are placed on people of various races and genders. It's also a good place to acknowledge that I am firmly in the category of "middle-aged White guy," well on my way to becoming "old White guy."

My experiences differ wildly from people of other races and genders. While my life is a neverending series of challenges, just like everyone else, there are additional doors and resources open to me that are not open to some others. While that belief has become very politically divisive, I can't in good conscience look at my life and the world around me without acknowledging the truth: My race and gender have made my life easier than others'.

Throughout the course of presenting these ideas to multiple groups, issues of race and gender quickly enter the conversation. If you are a person of color or a woman, an entirely different set of expectations is presented to you from the outside world. I cannot imagine bearing the weight of those expectations.

It was pointed out to me that I have no idea what it's like to be the only Black woman in a room. This is true. The only thing *I* need to belong in that room is a certain skill level, and even then, I can get away with less than others. Because I'm White and male, the bar is pretty low for me to clear. My presence in that room is *normal*. A Black female in the same room has to prove that they are not only smart enough, but that they are well *beyond* smart enough. They may feel the need to conform to societal expectations of how a Black woman should operate in a professional leadership capacity. Their bar is far higher than mine because a Black woman in that same room is *not* the norm.

There is also the weight that comes with feeling that one must represent every woman or every person of color who doesn't have a chance to be in the same room. This can be seen as either an honor or a burden (or both), but either way, it comes with weight.

My question is this: Do you actually *have* to accept those expectations?

Is the best way to represent your race or gender to try to conform to the expectations of society, or is it to show up as the most authentic version of yourself? When you operate from authenticity, you are showing up in a way that will *shine*. When you walk into a room with nothing to prove, you can truly serve others — because you are not trying to serve external expectations. This goes back to identity. Who are you at your best? That is the version of you this world needs more of, without the framework of external, and often ignorant, expectations getting in the way.

I am happy to be challenged to explore this topic further because I acknowledge I am viewing this through the lens of my experiences and the stories of others. Where I have landed so far is here: Everyone who has challenged me is a beautiful human being, who can have *more* impact when they aren't limited by the expectations of others. If you have strong thoughts on this section, I would genuinely love to hear your story and have a conversation (chad@forwardpartners.net).

I believe the lives of everyone around you will be better if you are able to reclaim these three elements of The Burnout Cycle: identity, expectations, and judgment. You can then show up as your authentic self — and change the world for the better. The world presents innumerable expectations to us. I believe we all have a choice as to whether or not we will let them dictate our lives.

The Perfection Trap

Another common trap we fall into as we chase unsustainable expectations is The Perfection Trap. When setting our goals or measures for success, we often expect that we will live up to them *perfectly*. Perfection then becomes its own unsustainable expectation.

New Year's resolutions are a great example of how perfection becomes a trap. We set our resolutions based on the assumption that we will perfectly live up to the plan. Sometimes that assumption of perfection is conscious, but it can also be unconscious. Either way, when we stumble, it all falls apart.

This is the year you are going to lose that stubborn weight that won't seem to go away. You design the perfect eating plan and commit to four workouts per week.

The first week, you knock it out of the park, actually enjoying the diet and working out each day with enthusiasm.

Week two, you accomplish everything, but it's a little harder. The low-calorie diet isn't as exciting and reality sets in — the gym suuuuuucks.

By week three, making it through these new routines is a real struggle, and you miss your first day at the gym. Because you started the day imperfectly, that evening you give in to the temptation of those Extra Toasty Cheez-Its and some MacAllan twelve-year-old scotch (yes, that's a *very* specific example — leave me alone). Half a box and a quarter bottle later, and your calorie count is blown.

Week four consists of a few more of those bad days. By week five, the gym is just a shame-generating memory and your diet looks better suited to a garbage disposal than to an actual healthy human being. Because of the shame generated by the failure, you actually gain *more* weight. Remember how you were going to do so well this year?

If perfection is ever part of your expectation — either consciously or unconsciously — then you are setting yourself up for failure because *perfection is never sustainable.*

Our identity and the unsustainable expectations we take on to prove we are okay are the first two elements in The Burnout Cycle. The third, judgment, now ensures that the Cycle continues unabated.

CHAPTER 7 REFLECTION

Reflection Questions

1. Which expectations in your life right now feel unreasonable, unattainable, unhealthy, or unwanted — and how are they draining your energy?

2. Where are you comparing yourself to "outliers" (like Spielberg at twenty-five, social media influencers, or unicorn start-ups), and how is that shaping your view of your own worth?

3. How does the Perfection Trap show up in your goals or daily
    routines, and what happens when you stumble?

....

....

....

....

....

....

Take Action

Make a list of five unsustainable expectations you currently
feel pressure to meet (from work, family, society, or yourself).
For each one, label it with one of the four "uns" (unreasonable,
unattainable, unhealthy, or unwanted). Then, choose one to begin
releasing this week by setting a healthier boundary or reframing
your measure of success.

CHAPTER 7 ENDNOTES

1. Benjamin Hardy and Dan Sullivan, *The Gap and The Gain: The High Achievers' Guide to Happiness, Confidence, and Success* (Hay House Business, 2021), 34.

"Judgments prevent us from seeing the good that lies beyond appearances."

— Dr. Wayne Dyer
author and speaker

Chapter 8

JUDGMENT

You Suck.

Judgment is useful only when it's aimed at our results, not at ourselves. Unfortunately, we rarely reserve judgment just for results. If the results are negative — not perfectly living up with unsustainable expectations — we judge *ourselves* as broken.

Evaluation and Condemnation

There are two types of judgment: evaluation and condemnation. Evaluation is about understanding. Condemnation is about guilt, shame, and blame. Evaluation is incredibly helpful. It is using judgment to better understand our results and next steps. However, condemnation happens when we begin to judge ourselves and not just our results.

The numbers aren't lacking. *I* am lacking.

The results aren't bad. *I* am bad.

The expectations we have chosen to take on become the

framework we use for judgment. When we take on unsustainable expectations, we judge ourselves using a set of rules and measures that are going to be challenging to live up to consistently. In the previous chapter, we looked at the four aspects of unsustainable expectations (unreasonable, unattainable, unhealthy, and unwanted). These will always consume an enormous amount of our limited energy. As our extra capacity is consumed, we are pushed closer to the brink of burnout.

We begin from a place of feeling like we are not enough and need to prove something. We adopt unsustainable expectations as a way to prove to ourselves and others that we are okay. The judgments we make of ourselves, based on these expectations, confirm our initial belief that we are broken or not enough. With that belief confirmed, we now have even more to prove, and so we take on even more unsustainable expectations, condemning ourselves to repeat The Burnout Cycle.

Stop Shoulding Yourself

The presence of the word "should" is evidence of a condemning judgment about ourselves, and probably indicates the existence of an unsustainable expectation.

I *should* be making more money.

I *should* be a better mother or father.

I *should* be further along.

Part of what makes unsustainable expectations so unsustainable is the condemning judgment that comes with them, which generates never-ending feelings of being behind. This feeling is often accompanied by fear and shame, which never enable positive long-term results.

When I hadn't created the equivalent of *Jaws* by the time I was twenty-five, I judged myself as being behind. This created shame and fear, which led me to … start my film career? No, it just led me to a lot of sulking and depression, and the belief that I was incapable of doing anything like that. None of those ingredients are part of the recipe for true success.

If you hear the word *should* in any of your thoughts about yourself, you can take it as a sign that you are judging *yourself* in a condemning way, not just evaluating your results.

The Gap and The Gain

In their book *The Gap & The Gain: The High Achievers' Guide to Happiness, Confidence, and Success,*[1] Benjamin Hardy and Dan Sullivan give us a valuable framework to understand if judgment is getting in our way. Are we living in The Gap or The Gain?

Often, we'll find ourselves in The Gap, a world where we are always comparing ourselves with an external expectation or ideal. When we compare ourselves to this ideal, we will often come up short, judging ourselves as broken. When we're in The Gap, everything that happens to us will *stop us* from getting to that ideal. It creates a negative lens through which we view, and judge, everything. When we're living in The Gap, we are always behind, and that will never change.

In The Gain, however, we never compare ourselves to an outside ideal. Instead, we only compare ourselves to where we have come from. In doing this, we are able to truly see the progress we are making. We begin to understand that everything that happens to us isn't a negative event designed to keep us from success. No, everything that happens is simply the next step on our road of progress. This gives us a more positive lens through which we can view everything. This view provides energy and excitement to fuel us on the journey.

Let's view my *Jaws* example through the lens of The Gap and The Gain. When I compared myself against Steven Spielberg (an outside ideal), I came up lacking and placed myself firmly in The Gap. This also meant everything around me was, in fact, stopping me from becoming the next Spielberg. Blessings like a growing family and a good job were all things holding me back from achieving my imagined destiny.

Had I been operating in The Gain, I would have only looked back. Despite my objective immaturity at age twenty-five, I had still come a long way. I was married at twenty-one, we had three awesome sons, I had started a business, and we had begun to figure out how to successfully be married. I was making progress and should have been deeply proud of that fact.

Instead of living with pride in our progress, I judged myself as being behind and wrestled with feelings of not being enough. All this amounted to increased unhappiness. My judgment of myself (rooted in unsustainable expectations) was confirming my beliefs about my brokenness and making me miserable.

Using the framework of The Gap and The Gain, you can tell if judgment is negatively impacting your view of yourself. Anytime you spot yourself living in The Gap, it's a sign you are in The Burnout Cycle and will need to do the work to reclaim these three elements — identity, expectations, and judgment.

Supportive Emotions vs. Barrier Emotions

Marcel Brunel and Dan Newby, in their book *Dignity in Policing: How Emotional Well-Being Saves Lives, Families, and Careers,*[2] dig into the idea of supportive emotions versus barrier emotions.

When the spotlight of judgment strays from our results to our identity, it opens the door to condemnation and shame. Shame is one of the top barrier emotions.

———

Barrier emotions impede effective functioning especially when we are under stress.

———

Barrier emotions cause us to show up in a more negative way, continuing to perpetuate the cycle of negative outcomes. Shame is often joined by embarrassment, guilt, fear, and resentment. With these emotions driving us, we are rarely making choices that are in our best interest. Instead, we are trying to assuage those feelings as quickly as we can. The fastest way to get rid of the shame of failure is to take on even larger expectations to prove we are doing just fine. But, of course, *taking on more unsustainable expectations is never the path to thriving.* To quote the great Zig Ziglar, "Don't do something permanently stupid because you're temporarily upset."

When we are able to separate judgment of results from judgment of our own identity, we can take advantage of supportive emotions.

———

Supportive emotions help reduce stress and promote healthy engagement.

———

Supportive emotions, like dignity, humility, honesty, gratitude, self-compassion, and determination, are available to us when we operate from an identity of wholeness — with nothing to prove.

Brunel and Newby write, "You need emotional literacy, which

is the ability to notice, name, and navigate your emotions."[3] When we can notice that we are experiencing barrier emotions, we can begin to realize we are probably trapped in The Burnout Cycle. We can then choose to do something about it.

"Just work harder"

The reason I sat at The Back Porch Intervention in 2010, staring at my own failure, was because I had allowed the three elements to keep me trapped in The Burnout Cycle. I *had* to fix my business because so much of my identity was tied into proving I could make it a success. I needed to prove to my wife, kids, and parents that their belief in me was justified. I needed to prove that I was okay.

Furthermore, I had embraced the unsustainable expectation that I make the business a success *on my own*. My own misconception of what strength really was kept me from asking for help. I had unconsciously taken on society's expectation that I appear strong no matter what, and I had run with it. This led to a total shut down of communication with the people around me — it led to isolation. All I had in those lonely moments of despair was my inner critic, which used comparison and judgment to show me just how broken I was.

When I would feel the shame of that judgment, I would circle back to my identity and feel like I *had* to prove I could do this. This cycle led to my continual overcommitment. The mantra "Just work harder" dominated my every waking moment. And because I never slept, there were *plenty* of those waking moments.

The mantra "Just work harder" proved to be an unsustainable expectation of its own. I expected that the quantity of hard work I was willing to do would yield success. I would embrace this expectation, adding another few hours of work to each day, awaiting success. When it never came, I would judge myself again, proving once more that I was broken. Wash, rinse, and repeat. The fact that I am here today to write these words is nothing short of a miracle. At the bottom of The Burnout Curve, the temptation to give up is tremendous.

Do Something About It

While The Burnout Cycle and The Burnout Curve are traps, they are *not* inescapable. We have the ability to escape the traps with intentional action. In Part 3, we'll learn about how stories dictate our experience of the world and how choosing better stories can change *everything*. We'll be able to reclaim those same three elements that are currently keeping us trapped: identity, unsustainable expectations, and judgment. Instead, we'll use these elements to create a version of ourselves that is truly capable of creating a better future.

CHAPTER 8 REFLECTION

Reflection Questions

1. Describe a time when your own unhealthy mindsets or actions
    caused you to react to a situation in an unhealthy way. How
    do you wish you had reacted differently?

2. Describe a situation when you can clearly remember going
    from a "get to" mindset to a "have to" mindset. Were you able
    to switch back to "get to" in that situation?

3. Describe a time when you felt so burned out (and probably
    alone) that you chose to give up on something that was
    potentially very good.

____

____

____

____

____

____

Take Action

For the next week, reflect at the end of each day and write down:

- One way you lived in The Gap today (comparing yourself
  to an external ideal).

- One way you lived in The Gain today (recognizing
  progress you've made).

Over time, you'll start to recognize when you are using judgment
in a negative way, and you'll intentionally focus on gratitude for
your progress instead.

CHAPTER 8 ENDNOTES

1. Benjamin Hardy and Dan Sullivan, *The Gap and The Gain: The High Achievers' Guide to Happiness, Confidence, and Success* (Hay House Business, 2021), 34.

2. Marcel Brunel and Dan Newby, *Dignity in Policing: How Emotional Well-Being Saves Lives, Families, and Careers* (Amz Marketing Hub, 2024).

3. Marcel Brunel and Dan Newby, *Dignity in Policing: How Emotional Well-Being Saves Lives, Families, and Careers* (Amz Marketing Hub, 2024), 103.

Part 3

ESCAPING THE TRAP

"The most powerful person in the world is the storyteller. The storyteller sets the vision, values, and agenda of an entire generation that is to come."

— Steve Jobs

Chapter 9

THE POWER OF STORY

The
Future

Everything about how we experience reality is a story. Stories are how our brains process the world around us. They not only determine how we see the world, but they also inform our every action.

All of the three elements of The Burnout Cycle (identity, unsustainable expectations, and judgment) are, in fact, stories. Your identity is the story you believe about yourself. Unsustainable expectations are stories about what we *should* be doing or not doing. Judgments are stories about our performance and potential. All of these stories combine to create our reality. Currently, they combine to create a reality where we are trapped in The Burnout Cycle.

Whether these stories are spoken out loud, or internally, they use language to shape how we see and experience everything. Language is how we, as humans, create the future. The exciting part about this is that stories can be *rewritten*. The future can be whatever we want it to be.

Creating with Language

In their book *The Three Laws of Performance: Rewriting the Future of Your Organization and Your Life*, Steve Zaffron and Dave Logan describe how powerful storytelling can be in leadership and in our lives. With their concepts of "the default future," "disempowered stories," and "future-based language,"[1] we see how stories can create reality. For a full look at Zaffron and Logan's concepts, I highly recommend their book. In this chapter and the next, I will explore how these concepts can help us rewrite our future.

The Default Future

The default future is the future we will experience, well, by default. It is the future created based on the stories that are currently running our view of reality. Most of these stories are created with "descriptive language." We are describing what we have experienced in the past and language creates the future; therefore, we will experience the same thing again. Combine that with our brain's habit of always finding what it's looking for, and you see how history can *literally* repeat itself.

Unfortunately, there is a major problem with our descriptions of the past: they aren't true. They are stories based on our narrow view of what happened. Visualize yourself sitting at a table with me and two other people. There is a bottle in the middle of the table. It has four vertical stripes, each a different color. From my perspective, the bottle is yellow because all I can see is the yellow stripe. From your perspective, the bottle is green because that is the only stripe visible on your side. Each of us experiences the same bottle, but we experience a different version of the bottle based on our perspective, and our history.

You might describe the bottle as hideous because green is your least favorite color. A kid in a green shirt bullied you once, and you've had a dislike for green ever since. I would describe the bottle as awesome because one of the primary colors for our company, Forward Partners, is yellow. I think our company is awesome, so by extension, I have a natural fondness for the bottle.

We all bring our past experiences and our narrow view of reality to the table to create a story about how we are experiencing something. This can impact our experience of an object (like the bottle), of a situation, or even of another person.

If we are in a conference room and Carl is presenting, I might have a very negative view of his presentation because he's *Carl* and I can't stand that guy (at this point, who can?). You might be enjoying the exact same presentation because Carl invited you to his wife's birthday party and you had a blast there.

Jennifer Moss writes, "An effective part of reframing involves examining the truth and accuracy (or lack thereof) of our stories. So, we need to ask, 'Are the things we're telling ourselves the absolute truth?'"[2]

We are each creating the future, which will look a lot like the past, based on stories that aren't fully true. Sounds a lot like The Burnout Cycle, doesn't it?

Disempowered Stories

When we are stuck in a loop of repeating history, we are dealing with a disempowered story. Because our actions are informed by the stories we believe, if we continue believing the same stories, we will continue to take the same actions. Despite taking all the same actions, we often expect different results. I think that's the definition of insanity.

When we're trapped in a disempowered story, it feels like we lack the ability to truly change. We'll experience repeated behaviors or choices that we don't like, and we won't really have hope they can be any different. This will be true of our experience of others, but most importantly, of our experience of ourselves. In the next chapter, we'll dive into how to unwind and rewrite disempowered stories.

Disempowered stories are easy to spot because they will usually relieve you of responsibility or make you feel superior to someone else. This is known as The Payoff, which we'll cover in more detail in the next chapter.

Let's use my favorite punching bag, Carl, as an example. I have a disempowered story in my head that Carl is an idiot. Why? Because one time he asked too many questions in a meeting and it led to a lot of extra work for me. This story is disempowered because it keeps me trapped in experiencing Carl only one way — as an idiot. Even thinking about Carl will cause me to experience frustration and impatience, which are barrier emotions robbing me of capacity. Is Carl an idiot at his core? No, of course not. However, I keep telling myself that story about him because it makes me feel superior. (I'm not an idiot, after all; therefore, I'm better.) It also relieves me of any responsibility to try to get to know him better and work with him as a colleague. I just get to sit and grumble about Carl. This disempowered story is hurting me every time I tell it, and it's preventing me from experiencing Carl as anything but an idiot.

I'll warn you up front that once you start noticing disempowered stories in your life, it will become frustrating. You will begin to understand just how much of your life is dictated by past experiences, and how little you have *intentionally* created. While it is frustrating, it is also the first step to opening the door to writing your own future.

Future-Based Language

Future-based language (or generative language) is how our ability to create the future with language transforms from a pattern-repeating curse into a superpower. We describe a new future which opens up new doors of possibility, allowing us to escape the trap of repeating history. It allows for a course of action that creates a different future.

When President John F. Kennedy declared, "We choose to go to the moon," he created a new future. Prior to this, visiting the moon was relegated to sci-fi novels. *There was no evidence it was even possible.* That declaration set the nation on a path of unparalleled innovation. He wrote that declaration using future-based language. This is the language of creation. Future-based language doesn't describe a past we've experienced. Instead, it describes a new future — it describes possibility. And because there doesn't have to be any evidence that this story is true, *it can be anything you want.*

Let's go back to Carl, the office idiot. The disempowered story is doing nothing positive for either Carl or me. Could we change my experience of him with future-based language? Let's try: Carl is an insightful, curious, and valuable member of the team.

Now, when we are sitting in the conference room at the end of a very long meeting and Carl raises his hand with more questions, I can choose the story I want to believe.

Carl is an idiot.

- I experience immediate resentment.

- Resentment turns into frustration and anger.

- I slam my laptop shut loud enough to draw irritated glances from the room.

Carl is an insightful, curious, and valuable member of the team.

- I recognize Carl as insightful and valuable.

- I experience curiosity myself; I'm interested to see where Carl's questions take us.

- I lean in, listening to his questions to see if I might find some insight from them.

It can't be that simple, right? Well, yes and no. Rewriting the future *is* that simple. Choosing to *believe* the new story will first require unwinding the disempowered story (which we'll cover in the next chapter), and then creating a practice of using the new story consistently. It's not a magical cure to our Carl-woes, but by doing the work, we will experience Carl differently.

Also bear in mind that whether Carl is *actually* an idiot or not doesn't matter. We aren't letting him off the hook for idiocy with this story. We're letting *ourselves* off the hook. We will change our experience of Carl, thereby lowering our stress level and enabling us to lead from a place of peace rather than frustration.

Stories About Who We Are

In the middle of writing this book, I was scheduled to have my first surgery. I had never experienced surgery in my life, so I was understandably nervous. I sat down in the pre-op room and they began taking my vitals.

"Oh, friend, your blood pressure is very high," the nurse said, looking worriedly at the monitor.

"That's not good," I said.

"No," she agreed, "It's really not."

She took my blood pressure a couple more times over the next half hour, and finally went to consult with the surgeon. The surgeon pulled back the tan curtain and sat down in front of me.

"I don't know how to tell you this," she began, "but we can't do your surgery today. I know that's not what you want to hear, but your blood pressure is dangerously high."

"Too high for surgery?" I asked.

"Maybe high enough to send you to the ER," she said.

I left the surgery center and visited an ER later that day. This led to subsequent visits to my doctor, who confirmed that I had high blood pressure and I needed to get it under control *fast*.

This was not really a great surprise to me. Up to that point, I had spent forty-five years abusing my body and doing very little to keep it healthy, like, you know, going to the doctor. While I've had fits and spurts of healthy living, they have never lasted. I needed this one to work. I understood there were probably some disempowered stories at the core of my seeming inability to consistently make healthy choices. I jumped on a call with my coach, Becky, and we began dissecting those stories and their origin.

Here are the stories I identified:

- *A healthy body is not for me.*

- *I am incapable of living a healthy life.*

Now, why would anyone believe that a healthy body was not for them? I had to go back to my childhood to figure that one out. When I was running around the kindergarten playground as a pint-sized He-Man, I first began to experience the story that a healthy body is not for me. I can remember beginning with comparison. I was tiny and scrawny. My classmates seemed like giants by comparison. That difference followed me all the way into middle and high school. As we began to age, other boys began to compare how their muscles were growing or how their veins stood out on their arms. Being physically behind everyone else, I didn't have big muscles or veins sticking out on my arms. I just assumed that those were not things I could ever have.

I tried soccer, baseball, and gymnastics in school. I was never gifted at any of them, while it seemed like everyone around me excelled. Therefore, I never really pushed myself to develop physically, not really working out until I was in my late thirties. I experienced all of these different things and they added up in my head to a simple truth: a healthy body is not for me.

That story led to actions like avoiding doctors, eating terribly, and not working out. And all of those actions led me to experiencing the second story — that I am incapable of living a healthy life. These two stories combined to influence negative actions over and over again, trapping me in a disempowered loop that led me to being fifty pounds overweight and wrestling with high blood pressure.

Those two simple stories about my identity created my reality. In order to continue living, I would have to unwind the disempowered stories and rewrite a new future for myself.

Disempowered Stories and Burnout

Just like disempowered stories created a cycle of unhealthy living for me, there will be disempowered stories that create a cycle of burnout for you. Disempowered stories can worm their way into every area of our lives. Our beliefs about ourselves, our value, our capabilities, other people, and situations all have the potential to be disempowered stories.

A disempowered story about needing to prove our value can easily lead to working through our vacations. A disempowered story about needing to be perfect can lead to additional stress on every project. A disempowered story about failure can lead to judging ourselves too harshly. Each of the lies we believe about the boulder is a disempowered story.

Spotting disempowered stories is step one in learning to defeat them. Now, we have to learn to unwind them or they will keep coming back to haunt us.

CHAPTER 9 REFLECTION

Reflection Questions

1. What disempowered stories do you repeatedly tell yourself about your identity, abilities, or relationships — and how have they shaped your actions and outcomes?

2. Where are you currently living in a default future — simply repeating past stories rather than intentionally creating a new one?

3. How do you think your life would look if burnout wasn't
    stealing your capacity?

....

....

....

....

....

....

....

Take Action

This week, notice one recurring negative pattern (e.g.,
procrastination, conflict with a person, unhealthy habit). Write
down the story you're telling yourself that fuels it.

CHAPTER 9 ENDNOTES

1. Steve Zaffron and Dave Logan, *The Three Laws of Performance: Rewriting the Future of Your Organization and Your Life* (Jossey-Bass, 2011).

2. Jennifer Moss, *The Burnout Epidemic: The Rise of Chronic Stress and How We Can Fix It* (Harvard Business Review Press, 2021), 174.

"Free yourself from the inauthenticity and disempowerment of your story."

— Steve Maraboli
author, athlete, and veteran

Chapter 10

UNWINDING DISEMPOWERED STORIES

R.I.P.

Here lies Chad.
He was horrible.

In *The Three Laws of Performance*, Zaffron and Logan break down the anatomy of a disempowered story, which they describe in three parts: complaint, payoff, and cost. Understanding these parts is important if we wish to unwind and replace our disempowered stories. When we don't break the cycle, these disempowered stories will maintain their hold on us, ensuring we repeat the future over and over again.

Anatomy of a Disempowered Story

The Complaint

Disempowered stories are often associated with an underlying complaint, so step one is to identify the complaint. Complaints are common in relationships, so let's start there. I have complained before that "Rebecca always makes us late to the movies."

Has this been true? Yes.

Is it *always* true? No.

And yet, every time we planned to go to the movies, I got mad *before* we were even ready to go. Sometimes, we weren't even late. But because I was operating with the story that "Rebecca always makes us late to the movies," I would deal with anger and frustration. And I was fully prepared to show how upset I was. The times when we weren't actually late, I would feel shame because I realized how unreasonable I was being. So, no matter what the outcome, that story changed my experience of going to the movies. Belief in that story created a version of me who was angry, frustrated, and sometimes filled with shame. One of my favorite places to be is the movie theater, and yet, I used to enjoy it a lot less because of this story.

Similarly, the complaint that "Carl is an idiot," spikes my blood pressure every time I think it (maybe Carl is the reason I have high blood pressure). That story makes me dread dealing with him, gossip about him, and avoid him at all costs. All of which makes *me* a bad teammate.

Has Carl been an idiot? Yes.

Is that who he truly *is*? No.

Is this story disempowered? Completely.

Think about some common complaints you have about yourself or someone else. Write down what the story is and see if you can find the parts that make it disempowered.

The Payoff

So why would we continue to tell ourselves these stories if they are clearly hurting us more than helping us? It's because there is a payoff to each story. Every time we tell ourselves the story, we get a payoff in the form of a dopamine hit or certain emotions. Disempowered stories almost always relieve us of responsibility or make us feel superior. However, there is usually some darkness to the payoff of a disempowered story. Let me demonstrate:

Rebecca always makes us late to the movies.

- I am relieved of the responsibility of being kind to her because she screwed up my enjoyment of a movie. This has led to some heated arguments before and after movies, and, if I'm being honest, I've said things that are just cruel.

- I'm relieved of the responsibility of being unselfish. If she's going to be *this* selfish, then clearly I have the right to be selfish, too.

- I feel superior because *I would never make us late.* I'm a world-class time manager. Does that make me a better human being? You bet your popcorn with extra butter it does. (Wait, maybe *that's* why I have high blood pressure.)

Now, hold on. Before you declare me to be an irredeemable monster, think through the story you wrote down as a complaint. Can you identify the payoff in that complaint? Does it somehow relieve you of responsibility or make you feel superior? If you can't identify the payoff in a disempowered story, then you'll be doomed to repeat that story — because that payoff makes it *just* sweet enough to keep telling it.

Write down any payoff you can identify for the complaint you wrote down.

The Cost

For every disempowered story, there is always a cost, and it can eventually become extreme. We keep telling ourselves the story and experiencing reality through that lens because we unconsciously enjoy the payoff, but the cost will eventually be due.

I will tell you that if you chase the cost list far enough, you will always land on someone dying. Let me show you. Start with the payoff to my story that "Rebecca always makes us late to the movies," and it's very easy to see the cost we will have to pay.

If I am relieved of the responsibility of being a kind, unselfish husband and believe I'm a superior human being, it will cost us.

- We will miss a fun trip to the movies because we'll argue the entire way there.

- We'll lose the desire to go on dates after a few of these experiences.

- As we stop dating one another, distance grows between us.

- We fight more and more often, making us both miserable.

- I become so unhappy that I meet another woman and begin an illicit affair.

- Rebecca finds out, murders me brutally, disposes of my body, and *gets away with it* because all she's been watching for years are true crime stories and *CSI*.

See? Dead. But let's pretend it doesn't go that far. Even if we stop at "we fight more and more often," I have still signed us up for misery — all because of one story. While that example might seem extreme, on a long enough timeline, similar stories and actions, played out consistently, can lead to results just like this. And this is just the potential cost of *one* disempowered story. Our reality is made up of an almost infinite number of stories.

Every time I walk someone through this exercise, they compare the payoff to the cost and it becomes obvious that continuing to live out the story is *not* worth it. Look at your complaint and the payoffs you identified. List out what that story could cost you if you continue to operate with it.

Once you see it written out, you have to pause and ask yourself, "Do I want to keep paying that cost?" If the answer is no, then you need to rewrite the story using future-based language rather than descriptive language.

Write it Down

I like to unwind disempowered stories using a whiteboard, but a piece of paper will do. There is something powerful about seeing the disempowered story in writing. It enables us to see the stark reality of it — it is hurting us. We can't deny the harm it is causing when we see a paltry list of payoffs and a lengthy list of costs.

Inevitably, people are uncomfortable to admit what they get from the payoff. I was uncomfortable writing about the example of Rebecca and me going to the movies. In writing, it's easy to see that I was not showing up as a good husband. And when I look at the potential cost, I feel sad and ashamed that I would subject us to that.

By writing it down, you are able to break apart the individual elements of the story and understand it more completely. Now, when the story pops up in your head, and it will again, you can stop and intentionally consider the cost. You can then decide if you are willing to pay the cost. If not, you can replace the disempowered story with a new future.

Rewriting the Story

Rewriting stories is going to come in handy when it comes to creating a new, burnout-free future, especially if you have felt like there is no hope of ever winning the battle. That disempowered story can be unwound and rewritten in a way that opens up entirely new doors for you — paths to health, growth, and impact.

You can write any future you want. This is the beauty of creation, you are creating from *nothing*. You are not creating by describing something you have experienced, which limits you. Instead, you are creating from an infinite number of possibilities.

What if my story "Rebecca always makes us late to the movies" shifted to "We are going to have a great time at the movies no matter when we arrive, because we are blessed to be together"? My story determines the version of me that shows up. Here's how the version of me that shows up will differ depending on the story:

Rebecca always makes us late to the movies.
- I am unkind.
- I am angry.
- I am selfish.
- I am cruel.
- I am arrogant.

We are going to have a great time at the movies no matter when we arrive, because we are blessed to be together.
- I am excited.
- I am patient.
- I am loving.
- I am charming.
- I am considerate.

It's easy to see which version of me will enjoy not just a good movie but also a long, happy marriage, and which version of me will end up chopped up into tiny pieces and buried in multiple coffee cans in a lonely desert in West Texas.

Look at your complaint, along with its payoffs and costs. What version of you does that create? Now rewrite an empowered version of that story — a new future — that will create a different version of you.

Using Empowered Stories

Once you have unwound the disempowered story into its individual parts and written a new story, it's time to use it. One hurdle will be muscle memory. Most disempowered stories have staying power because humans are habitual creatures. You will have believed some of these stories for so long, that it will take a while to replace them fully, especially when you first begin this work.

A long-held disempowered story will continue to show up in your mind even after you have unwound it. Your job, when you notice it, will be to replace it with the empowered story. Sometimes it's helpful to even speak it out loud.

If Rebecca and I are preparing to go to the movies and I feel my old frustration show up, I can either give in to it and pay the cost, or I can *choose* my empowered story. When I hear "Rebecca always makes us late to the movies," my job is to notice it, stop, and make a *conscious choice*. Out loud, I can say, "We are going to have a great time at the movies no matter when we arrive, because we are blessed to be together."

The beauty of a positive and empowered story is that it generates excitement for the future. There will be times when the empowered story has to be repeated quite a few times in order to overpower the built-in strength of the disempowered story.

You might also find some disempowered stories to be especially stubborn, burrowing into the deepest folds of your brain and refusing to acknowledge the eviction notice you are giving them. In these cases, it might be necessary to not only do the internal work, but to employ external help as well.

This is where having support from fellow leaders is helpful. When I am struggling with a particularly relentless disempowered story, I often tap members of my Circle of Support (a concept we will explore more fully in Chapter 16). I will lay out for them how the disempowered story is keeping me trapped, share the empowered story I would rather operate with, and then I will ask for accountability and support.

Whether you overcome the disempowered story through repetition of an empowered story or by employing external support, the point is to make sure you overcome it. Winning the battle against burnout will *require* empowered stories.

We were recently on a trip to Aspen, Colorado, where I facilitated a retreat. The five-hour trip home turned into a forty-eight-hour travel debacle that we could make a movie about. Whatever could go wrong, did go wrong — multiple airplane mechanical issues, multiple canceled flights, an airport closure, plus extra rental car and hotel costs.

When the first flight was canceled, it was clear to me that everyone around me was having a *really* bad time. I could feel myself being sucked into the negativity swirling around me. I heard all kinds of disempowered stories about airlines and the idiots running them. At that point, I didn't know what lay ahead of us over the next two days. What I did know was that I didn't want to spend the rest of my trip angry. I intentionally wrote an empowered story, right there in the airport: We're on an adventure.

I could see all the delays and challenges through a

disempowered lens that would only generate frustration and anger. That was clearly what was happening to everyone around me.

Instead, I chose to see it as an adventure. It was a huge blessing that we got to work in Colorado in the first place. Being able to fly across the country is normal for modern Americans, but when viewed through the lens of history, it's a *miracle*.

There I stood, in the long line, to reschedule our first of several canceled flights. In line, I was relaxed and happy, while everyone around me was angry and worried. Why? Because I was on an adventure. The people around me clearly *were not*. I listened as they yelled at the people who were doing their best to help us. I watched one woman scream into her phone, "LET ME TELL YOU WHY I'M NOT FLYING ACROSS THE ENTIRE COUNTRY IN F\${&!#G COACH!" She wasn't having a good time.

When my turn at the counter finally came, I greeted the harried attendant with a big smile. "Hey," I said, "my goal right now is to be the best customer you deal with all day."

She gave a relieved smile back and said, "Thank you. Let's see if we can get you taken care of."

That was the first of many great interactions I would have with travel professionals in four cities across two states in forty-eight hours. Each one was great because of how I showed up, which was based on an empowered story that I *chose*.

Because of that choice, I actually enjoyed what could have been a very bad experience. Rebecca and I still laugh about how much fun we had hanging out together in the airports. Every time something new would go wrong, I would look at her, smile, and say, "Adventure."

The adventure finally concluded on day three when my luggage arrived at our front door step. It had missed one of our replacement connecting flights and had to be hand delivered. Can I be honest? I was a little sad when it showed up. I hauled it through the front door and told Rebecca, "Well, I guess the adventure is finally over."

In every situation we experience, we get to choose the story we believe, and thereby choose the version of us that exists in that moment. It can transform any experience, which is a powerful way to live life.

Look at the empowered story you have rewritten. You've taken a disempowered story, broken down its components to really understand it, and written a new future. Now it's time to practice repeating that empowered story over, and over, and over again. This will enable you to show up at your best and intentionally create that future.

I am Designed to Live a Long, Healthy Life

Having identified disempowered stories about my own health, I had to unwind them and rewrite them, or overcoming this blood pressure problem would never be a reality for me. Here's what that looks like:

Complaint:
- A healthy body is not for me.
- I am incapable of living a healthy life.

Payoff:
- I am relieved of the responsibility of having to keep my body healthy (plus, I save time by not going to the gym).
- I am relieved of guilt when I make unhealthy choices (I'm looking at you, pizza and scotch).

- I am superior to people who have healthy bodies, because look at all I'm accomplishing *despite* being broken.

Cost:

- I don't create a consistent habit of going to the gym.
- I see any challenging event as an excuse to make poor food and drink choices.
- I gain more weight.
- My blood pressure continues to go up.
- My family history of diabetes suddenly becomes a reality for me.
- My quality of life continues to plummet.
- My life ends after a debilitating stroke, heart attack, or diabetic complications.

Stories that began in my childhood with bullying and comparison to others had united to keep me from taking consistent action for myself. As I look at that list of costs, I realize that they have been very clearly demonstrated to me. When I think about my extended family, I can't think of anyone who was incredibly healthy to the end, enjoying what life had to offer all the way to their last day. No, I see story after story of people whose bodies slowly wasted away, each enduring tremendous pain until the heart breaking, and entirely predictable, end.

Understanding these disempowered stories more clearly, I was ready to rewrite mine. I did so with three distinct stories, using future-based language — describing a future of new possibilities.

I am:

- Designed to live a long, healthy life.
- Proud of every aspect of my body.
- A perfect physical example for other people.

"Wait, wait, wait," I hear you saying, "I've seen you. You are not a *perfect* physical example for other people, Big Guy."

But remember, the empowered story comes from nothing and requires zero evidence of existence. You can create *anything you want*. And this matters because what you are really creating is the version of you that will exist to take action.

Stop and think about the choices, actions, and viewpoints that are easy for someone who is designed to live a long, healthy life, who is proud of their body, and who is a perfect physical example for other people. They will be more consistent with their healthy choices. The gym will be exciting instead of daunting. Healthy food is delicious. Soreness is a sign of progress. Saying no to bad foods is easier.

I began using these new stories, looking at them and reciting them out loud each day. I found all the things above to be *true*. I don't have to actually see evidence of being a perfect physical example in order to live like one. I simply have to believe the story that this is who I am at my core (underneath all the fat).

As I make choices in line with someone who deserves a long, healthy life, I am actually living that life. And even though the weight is dropping off me rapidly, I'm not proud of some future version of my physical body. I'm proud of it today. Even though I'm not where I eventually want to be, I've noticed more feelings of pride when I look in the mirror.

I choose to live the life of a healthy person by embracing *empowered* stories about who I am and what I'm capable of. For the first time in forty-five years, I feel like I have a handle on my own health and what I will be capable of in the future.

Dan Sullivan and Benjamin Hardy speak to this idea in their book, *10x Is Easier Than 2x: How World-Class Entrepreneurs Achieve More by Doing Less*: "The most fundamental qualitative change is internal, your vision and identity. By changing these, everything else you're doing simultaneously changes as well. You take your internal and emotional evolution and externalize that in the form of refined standards and results."[1]

CHAPTER 10 REFLECTION

Reflection Questions

1. What recurring complaint do you often voice (about yourself, others, or circumstances), and how might it actually be a disempowered story?

2. What payoff are you secretly getting from this story?
    Does it let you avoid responsibility, or make you feel superior in some way?

3. What is the real cost of holding onto this story long term, and do you honestly want to keep paying that price?

Take Action

Unwind one disempowered story that is causing you to repeat negative patterns. Write down the complaint, payoff, and cost. Then write a new future for yourself with an empowered story.

CHAPTER 10 ENDNOTES

1. Dan Sullivan and Benjamin Hardy, *10x Is Easier Than 2x: How World-Class Entrepreneurs Achieve More by Doing Less* (Hay House Business, 2023), 14-15.

"Life is not about finding yourself. Life is about creating yourself."

— George Bernard Shaw

Chapter 11

RECLAIMING YOUR IDENTITY

It took the first ten chapters to set up the problem and learn about stories. Now it's time to really get to work winning the battle against burnout. You've learned how to rewrite disempowered stories. Next, you'll learn to write new stories to reclaim the three elements that keep you trapped — identity, expectations, and judgment. We'll begin with your identity.

Your True Identity

When you operate from completeness — being at your best — you can make intentional choices to create the life you want, free of the need to prove or punish. Stop and think of all the energy in your life that has gone into trying to prove that you were enough. Think of every bit of energy you've spent worrying about whether or not other people think you are enough. And it's not just energy, but time and money as well.

Now imagine all those resources *reinvested* in creating a future where you are able to live your life on your terms, serving others and having Sustainable Impact. Don't think about all that with regret. Just know it was a part of your journey to this point — this very moment — and *now* you can begin to intentionally create a better future.

As Sullivan and Hardy wrote, "The scariest and most exciting thing you'll ever do is be your truest self, holding nothing back, and with no apology."[1]

Your true self is not broken.

Your true self is enough.

It's time to set your true self free.

Recognizing Misalignment

The truth of your identity — that you are enough — is a North Star that you must stay aligned with in order to operate as your most impactful self. Staying aligned with the truth is a challenge because it's a moment-to-moment practice, and many things conspire to knock you out of alignment, including burnout. Because you have received so many messages throughout your life that you are not enough, it's very easy for your brain to latch onto that belief. It's a story your mind has believed for most of your life, so it can be comforting in a darkly familiar way. Returning to stories that you are broken or not enough might be the strongest muscle memory you have.

If your mind latches on to stories of brokenness, you will operate out of brokenness once again. You will go from making intentional choices to create the life you want, to shouldering unsustainable expectations to try and prove your worth. This is where burnout will take over and ensure the misalignment continues.

———

*Burnout is the loss of capacity to align with your
purpose, do your most sacred work, and enjoy life.*

———

The first step to reclaiming your identity is recognizing when you
are out of alignment with the truth. Here are three questions you
should be consistently asking yourself:

Do I feel like I'm not enough or broken?

Do I feel the need to prove anything?

Do I feel the need to hide or punish myself?

When I notice anxiety, I stop and ask the first question. When
I operate from a place of completeness, my anxiety level will be
much lower. For me, anxiety is usually a sign that I don't feel like
I'm enough in whatever situation I'm experiencing.

Prior to walking into any meeting, I like to ask myself the
second and third questions. If I feel like I have to prove something
in a room, then I know I will not be entirely of service to others.
Any service I give will be to prove that I belong or to impress.
That's not true service to others because it's ultimately self-
serving.

If I answer yes to the question about hiding or punishment,
it usually means I have believed the story that I am not enough
and I want to hide from others so they won't also realize that I'm
broken. It is also a signal to be hyper-intentional with my actions
going forward because the need to punish will often lead to poor
choices.

If we can answer yes to any of the three questions, it is a
sign that we are no longer aligned with the truth. We are then

operating with disempowered stories, and the version of us that is showing up is not as impactful as it could be.

Realigning with the Truth

To realign with the truth of who you are, disempowered stories need to be replaced with empowered stories.

Think of yourself as a computer. Whatever base programming is in your operating system will determine what the computer does. When your operating system is based on a disempowered story, you will function according to whatever that disempowered story dictates. Realigning with the truth is an exercise in resetting the programing to baseline and then adding in new code.

Part 1 - Returning to Baseline

Returning your internal computer to baseline involves writing a new story. The truth — you are enough — is that story. Here is a simple statement to remind yourself of the truth:

"I am whole, complete, and there is nothing wrong with me. I am enough."

The first time you say it out loud to yourself, The Bullshit Response we discussed in Chapter 6 will most likely happen. Your mind will try to reject the thought because it doesn't line up with what it is already looking for — brokenness. Repeat the phrase out loud. "I am whole, complete, and there is nothing wrong with me. I am enough." Repeat the phrase as many times as you need to, until you finally feel a sense of excitement or peace. For me, I can feel it in my chest. It's a relieving of tension, as if something is unlocking inside me.

The first time my coach, Becky, had me work through this exercise, I thought it was really dumb. The Bullshit Response was *strong*. I said the phrase out loud, "I am whole, complete, and there is nothing wrong with me. I am enough." In addition to literally saying, "bullshit," I laughed. I repeated it out loud a second time, and The Bullshit Response was the same.

I sat there in my car, repeating the phrase out loud, over, and over, and over again. Somewhere around the thirtieth time, I felt the tightness in my chest release and I was able to breathe deeper. I felt an odd peace.

This is where the computer that dictates how we show up has zeroed out all the disempowered code and has returned to its baseline. It understands that we are enough and it's no longer trying to reject that idea. Now it is ready for new code.

Part 2 - "I Am" Statements

You will write this new code with "I am" statements. These statements will be instructions for your subconscious, telling it which version of you it should create. Stop and think about what version of you will be most effective in whatever you do next. Describe that future version of you beginning with "I am."

I have a list that I use consistently. It describes who I am when I'm at my best, which is really who I am at my core. "I am whole, complete, and there is nothing wrong with me. I am enough."

I Am:

- *Hope*
- *Clarity*
- *Generosity*
- *Patience*
- *Connection*
- *Inspiration*
- *Determination*
- *Focus*
- *Energy*
- *Love*
- *Life*

These statements serve as new instructions for my subconscious mind, which will then go to work creating that version of me. Your list can look the same, or wildly different. The key is that it's *your* list. In Chapter 6, you wrote down what you look like at your best. Many of the words for this list will come from that description of yourself.

We zeroed out our subconscious programming by repeating aloud the statement, "I am whole, complete, and there is nothing wrong with me. I am enough." For these "I Am" statements, we will use our voice as well. Once you have your list and have returned to baseline, repeat your list out loud. This action tells your subconscious what you want to be in order to show up as your best self.

Programming yourself this way isn't about *doing*, it's about *being*. It's about embodying all these traits in such a way that the other people in the room can't help but experience something special. They will experience a version of you who is truly of service to them because you aren't weighed down with the burden of needing to prove anything. They will experience you as your most authentic self.

Living and serving as our authentic selves is exciting for everyone around us because we show up and *create*. We begin by creating the best version of ourselves and then proceed to create a new future for others as well. This enables us to serve our purpose — positively impacting the people around us. We begin to see new levels of impact and view our everyday work through the lens of sacred work.

When I operate from my true self, I experience pride, excitement, love, and hope. But it is a non-stop practice to maintain my alignment with my true self. I'm consistently asking the three questions to recognize if I'm out of alignment, then returning to baseline, and reminding myself who *I am*.

Eventually the exercise takes very little time and can be done right after a tough meeting, right before starting an important presentation, or prior to walking in the front door after a difficult day. The first time I did this, it took me thirty-plus times to feel anything. Now I can usually repeat the phrase once and that's all it takes. I've done it for so long that The Bullshit Response has been replaced with an excited, "Let's go!" As you do this exercise on a regular basis, the same will be true for you.

I usually begin every day by ensuring my subconscious computer is properly programmed. I answer two simple questions:

1.   *What am I committed to creating today?*

2.   *What version of me needs to show up to fulfill that commitment?*

I remind myself of the truth of my completeness and that I am capable of creating anything. The commitment in question one determines the direction of my day. Then, based on my answers to question two, I'll speak "I Am" statements to provide the proper instructions. This exercise creates the best version of me — who I truly am — to show up and serve. From there, I monitor how I'm doing throughout the day, and if I spot any misalignment, I'll take intentional action to fix it. Sometimes it is a short pause, a quick call to someone I trust, or a walk around the block to realign myself.

I would love to hear how this works for you and learn what your "I Am" statements look like (chad@forwardpartners.net).

CHAPTER 11 REFLECTION

Reflection Questions

1. When do you most often slip into disempowered stories about being broken, needing to prove yourself or hiding? What triggers those stories?

2. How would your life be different if all the energy you've spent proving or hiding was reinvested into creating a future aligned with your true self?

3. Which "I Am" statements feel most authentic to you when you
    picture yourself at your best?

....

....

....

....

....

....

Take Action

Each morning, repeat out loud: *"I am whole, complete, and
there is nothing wrong with me. I am enough."* Expect The
Bullshit Response at first. Keep repeating until you feel even a
small shift toward peace or excitement. This resets your inner
operating system to truth. Create your personal list of five to ten
"I Am" statements that describe who you are at your best. Speak
them out loud daily — especially before stressful meetings, hard
conversations, or walking into your home after a long day. This
programs your subconscious to bring your true self forward.

CHAPTER 11 ENDNOTES

1. Dan Sullivan and Benjamin Hardy, *10x Is Easier Than 2x: How World-Class Entrepreneurs Achieve More by Doing Less* (Hay House Business, 2023), 125.

"Commitment is
what transforms
a promise
into reality."

— Abraham Lincoln

Chapter 12

RECLAIMING EXPECTATIONS

MAYBE?

In the Burnout Cycle, we operate from brokenness and take
on expectations to prove we are enough. When we are aligned
with the truth, and don't need to prove anything, we are free.
Unfortunately, we will be prone to giving that freedom up because
expectations will still be placed on us, and our muscle memory
is strong. To stop the Burnout Cycle, we need a framework to
evaluate those expectations, determine if they line up with what
we want, and *choose* to either take them on or reject them.

To begin, we will need to create agreements. These are contracts
we make with ourselves and those around us about what we
want to create. Agreements differ from expectations in their
effectiveness. Almost every leadership book will tell you that
you must set clear expectations for your people. Expectations
are wildly inefficient when they are from an external source. The
pattern below illustrates the inefficiency of external expectations.

When we first take on the expectations, we will briefly live up to them. However, if we don't fully buy into them, which is common with external expectations, we will eventually fall off and our consistency dips. Eventually, someone reminds us of the expectations, usually with shame, and we live up to them again — but only briefly. This pattern causes inefficiency and keeps us trapped in The Burnout Cycle. Whether it's an expectation we have placed on ourselves or one someone else has given to us, we must expend continual effort to get back on track when we stray.

Agreements differ in that they are something we *desire*. When we agree, we are contracting with ourselves to achieve an outcome by doing, or not doing, certain things. Internal agreements will beat external expectations every time. Rather than sapping our energy like unsustainable expectations, agreements will become a framework for what we want our lives to look like.

Commitment vs. Involvement

Agreements are effective because they are internal desires. They work because of our commitment to them. The reason expectations are so inefficient is because we are rarely committed to them; instead, we are merely involved.

The best way to illustrate the difference between commitment and involvement is with the old fable about the chicken and the pig. If you have eggs and bacon for breakfast, the chicken was involved in your breakfast, whereas the pig was *fully committed*. The chicken got up that morning, laid a few eggs, and then went chickening around for the rest of the day. The pig gave the ultimate sacrifice for you to enjoy that crispy, salty, bite of Heaven.

In every situation, are you the chicken or the pig? Are you involved as long as it is convenient, easy, and rewarding? Or are you committed — mind, body, and soul — to living up to the agreement? Commitments are easy to make and difficult to live up to. The more we learn to have integrity with our commitment, especially commitments to *ourselves*, the more we will build trust. Commitments matter and should not be made lightly. However, when you do make a commitment, *be the pig*.

Creating Agreements

When we truly begin to live aligned with the truth of our identity — that we're badasses — we can begin to clear out all the old expectations that have eaten our time and energy. This will leave us with a reserve of capacity that needs to be directed, which leads us to agreements. Agreements will ensure we are creating the life we *want*, not living it according to someone else's desires. Agreements need to be established in three primary areas: you, your family, and your work.

We're going to start with three basic questions. These are not always questions you'll have answers to immediately. I would recommend taking some time, perhaps even weeks, to really ponder these questions for yourself.

What do I want to create for myself?

What do I want to create for my family?

What do I want to create through my work?

Once you identify what you want to create in each area, there will be a few other questions to ask to ensure you have the capacity to live up to your commitments:

What new rhythms do I need to embrace?

What new boundaries do I need to establish?

What accountability needs to be put into place to ensure I stay on track when I stumble?

As you think through what you want to create, it's a good idea to involve the people who will be affected. The art of co-creation ensures more buy-in from everyone involved. Write what you want to create for your family and then invite them to the conversation. If you are married or in a relationship, it's deeply important that you both agree on what you want to create. Otherwise, you will constantly find yourself at odds with one another.

As you decide what you want to create at work, involve your bosses. Through that, you may find that your goals are not aligned with the company's, or that it isn't the place where you can create what you want. The old you might stay at the company indefinitely in order to prove you were a good employee. The new you, with nothing to prove, has the freedom to choose. If you stay, make that choice because it aligns with what you want to create. If you leave, make that choice because it will allow you to fulfill your commitments to yourself. Either way, choose for yourself, not because of external expectations.

Now, let's look at each of the three areas of creation.

You

This list intentionally begins with you. We are often taught to put ourselves last because otherwise we are selfish. The key is understanding that any investment in yourself will pay dividends for your family and in your work. *You are always your best investment.*

Billionaire Warren Buffet knows a thing or two about investment, and he agrees: "The best investment you can make is yourself." Motivational speaker Brian Tracy says, "An investment in self-development pays the highest dividends."

Most of us have spent our lives trying to live up to expectations and wasting so much of our capacity. Intentionally creating the life you want is far more about efficient use of your resources — focusing them where they can do the most good.

So, the questions stand:

What do you want to create for yourself?

What would you agree to create if you had nothing to prove to anyone?

What would you invest to gain new skills, abilities, or experiences?

What have you always wanted to do?

Begin to write out an agreement with yourself about what you want to create. Use all the questions we've discussed to provide the framework for that agreement.

Your Family

I spent far too long unintentionally leading my family. I was not trying to create anything in particular, I was merely trying to survive. Proverbs 29:18 says, "Where there is no vision, the people perish." Whether you believe in the Bible or not, this proverb has proven historically true over and over. As human beings, we need a North Star. We need a purpose bigger than ourselves — a vision to live for.

Without that, we simply exist.

We just survive.

But, we want to *thrive*.

This requires agreements about what we want to create for our family. Think ahead a decade.

Other than older, what do you want your family to be like? How do you want your relationship with your significant other to look and work?

What do you want your relationship with your children and extended family to be like?

What do you want to create?

If you don't intentionally create this vision and agree to create it together, you will simply live out the default future, repeating patterns. And if you chose this book in the first place, I'm guessing those will be patterns like The Burnout Cycle. I can tell you from firsthand experience that repeating *that* cycle over and over again will do nothing but create hurt, sadness, distance, fear, and shame.

Your family will most likely be the biggest part of your legacy that you leave behind. Be intentional with creating a family legacy that they are proud to be a part of.

Your Work

Work is where most people will spend the majority of their waking lives. At work, our focus is often on what's *next*. From the next promotion, to the next raise, to the next sale, to the next project, to the next quarter. To quote the great philosopher Yoda, "All his life he has looked away … to the future, to the horizon. Never his mind on where he was. Hmm? What he was doing." [1]

When work is only about what's next, we often fall into the trap of believing that what's next will finally be satisfying or make us happy. I promise you that if your last promotion didn't satisfy you, the next one won't either. Instead of focusing on next, we should focus on creating impact.

Outside of your family, your work will give you the most opportunity to have a deep impact on the lives of others. From your coworkers to the customers you serve, when you show up as your truest self, you can't help but positively impact the people around you. When you operate as your authentic self, you change the energy in every room you walk into. You will learn that by being *you*, you are able to create entirely new outcomes.

What outcomes would you like to create at work — if anything were possible? If you had no fear of failure, what would you create in your professional life? The answer to those questions could change the course of your career path by opening entirely new doors, or it could deepen the impact you have on your current path. Either way, you will learn the joy of showing up every day to have a positive impact on others. Nothing will fuel you more than that.

Accountability and Communication

Accountability will be a key part of successfully living up to an agreement. When you make an agreement and commit to it, you will almost immediately screw it up. This is human nature. What has to be built into the agreement is a mechanism for accountability. When you or someone else violates the agreement, how will you handle it? Violations of the agreement will happen. Agree now on how to get back on track.

Once you have created agreements about anything, it's key that you obtain commitment from everyone that is a part of the agreement. Again, reiterate the difference between involvement and commitment. Are they willing to be the pig? If not, you will experience some painful friction in the future.

When you are living by the agreement, it's vital that you communicate about it often. Even committed pigs will sometimes stray from the path. A regular check-in about the agreement keeps it fresh in everyone's minds. This is also a good place to measure progress of your new creation. As you move forward with your agreement, you'll experience both wins and setbacks. It's important to celebrate the wins as markers of progress. These will provide fuel for the creation process.

I No Longer Agree to This Agreement

Let's pretend you have created an agreement with your spouse about building a business together. You both agree to keep your full-time jobs, work on the business in the evenings, and slowly build it to profitability. Two years into this journey, you have both consistently lived up to your commitment, but you have also found that you don't actually enjoy owning a business. Is it okay to break your commitment to the agreement?

Absolutely. The point of agreements is so everyone can move forward together, creating the life you *want*. If you discover on the path that you no longer want what you thought you did, it's time for a new agreement. The agreement is a framework for success, but you are free to change games if you decide the one you are currently playing isn't fulfilling anymore.

In that case, come together with your spouse, agree to nullify the agreement, and start working on your next agreement. Being the pig doesn't mean mindlessly following our agreements. We have to constantly assess if the agreement is still workable for us.

If it turns out the agreement we made is leading to burnout, then we can reevaluate it and make changes.

Using Agreements to Evaluate Expectations

Learning to live aligned with truth and by agreements doesn't mean that expectations are entirely a thing of the past. Part of creating a new life will involve excavating parts of your old life. You will inevitably dig up some expectations that have to be dealt with. You will also have new expectations placed on you, both internally (because it's the way you have operated for so long) and externally (because that's the way the world operates).

Your agreements give you a framework to evaluate the expectations and decide if you want to live by them. We have to start by spotting expectations. As we discussed in previous chapters, expectations will usually come with the words "expect" or "should." When you hear those words, it's a sign for you to instantly focus on what's being said. Whether it's a voice in your head or the directive from your boss, you need to pause and evaluate the expectation with a few questions.

Does this expectation line up with what I have agreed to create?

Is this expectation unsustainable?

Am I willing to truly commit to this expectation? Am I the chicken or the pig?

If the expectation lines up with what you want to create, is sustainable, and you are truly willing to commit, incorporate it into your current agreements, or make a new one. This is you consciously choosing what you want.

Is your boss, spouse, client, or child going to hand you an expectation that you don't want to take on? Sure. They will often give you expectations that don't work for you. They might not line up with what you are creating or fit who you are. They might be unsustainable. In those moments, the yes or no is still yours. Stop and ask the misalignment questions from Chapter 11.

Do I feel like I'm not enough or broken?

Do I feel the need to prove anything?

Do I feel the need to hide or punish myself?

If the answer to any of these is yes, go back and do the mindset work to realign with the truth — you are enough and have nothing to prove. Now look at the expectation again. Do you have the strength to have a tough conversation about it? When you are operating from truth, you will find the energy to have a challenging conversation about why you are unwilling to live up to an expectation. When you are trying to please the people around you (trying to prove something), that conversation will rarely happen.

Do we ever take on unsustainable expectations as a path toward what we want to create? Sometimes. Let's pretend what you want to create in your work life is a new role at a new company that is better for you. Your current boss brings you an expectation — let's say a project that will require eighty man-hours but must be done in the next week — do you say yes to it? First, I would ask for more time or more help. But, ultimately, *if keeping this job is part of what will help me create my new one,* I would probably say yes. Notice we're not committing to do ten of these. However, there are times when we can take on unsustainable expectations to achieve a short-term goal. We simply have to make sure there are boundaries on that unsustainable expectation, and that living up to it will contribute to the future we want to create.

At Forward Partners, we generally limit our weeks for forty hours or less. When combined with rest, this is a very sustainable rhythm. However, there will be times, like in preparation for the launch of this book, when we will work significantly more. We are agreeing to commit to fifty hours per week for a *limited time* to achieve a short-term goal. When you first have a baby, you are committing, for a time, to a very unsustainable sleep schedule. There are limited times we say yes, in service to creating a better future.

Clearing Out Old Unsustainable Expectations

You will often spot unsustainable expectations when you identify disempowered stories in your life. When you find an old expectation that has been running your life, it's not enough to just say, "I'm enough, I don't have to prove anything anymore." That is akin to Michael Scott from *The Office* saying in a loud voice, "I declare bankruptcy!" and believing it actually did anything. Clearing out old expectations will be an ongoing process and usually involves difficult conversations with the source of those expectations — either you or someone else.

Let's pretend your parents created an expectation that you bring your family over every Sunday for lunch and an afternoon filled with board games. This is something you have done for years, at first because you wanted to, but recently out of guilt.

But now, you have created agreements about what you want to create for yourself and your family. You have decided to go back to school and get your master's degree, and your son has committed to playing baseball every Saturday. These two agreements are now eating up your weekends.

If family lunch no longer aligns with what you are creating, you have two choices: You can continue to operate with the unsustainable expectation that you are there every Sunday, like clockwork, probably pushing your school work to the evening and eating up what little rest time you have. Or you can sit Mom and Dad down, explain what you have agreed to create, and let them know that for this season you will not be at family lunch. If Mom and Dad respond negatively, it will be a good time to do a truth alignment check. Nothing will make us feel like we are *not* enough faster than the shame and guilt parents can intentionally or unintentionally dole out. If that happens, hold the line. This is about creating your life, not just experiencing the repeated life everyone else wants you to have.

With every expectation you uncover, and again it's a never-ending process, you will be required to operate from a place of wholeness to have some tough conversations.

Agreeing with the Disagreeable

Is it possible to create an agreement with a person who is unwilling to participate? No. Does this create some real challenges? Yes.

Often the people who refuse to participate are people who are dearest to us. They are not in a place in their lives to recognize the potential good of creating a new future. Or they're afraid of change. Or they're just plain old stubborn. Either way, you might have some difficult decisions to make.

The first agreements you make are with yourself. What do *you* want to create? Are you willing to be the pig? You'll have to line up what you want to create with what they want to create, and see where you might need to be flexible. This will also help you

identify what parts of your vision for the future are absolutes for
you. What parts are you totally unwilling to budge on?

"Well the person in my life doesn't want to create *anything*."
In a way, they are still creating, it's just not a *new* future. It's the
same one they have been trapped in (probably for a while). Not
everyone is in a place to do this work. It took me a lot of therapy
to be open to the idea that I had the ability to create a brighter
future. Maybe they haven't done that work or are unwilling
to. Now you have to decide if you will remain trapped with
them. Either way, you are making a choice, which is still better
than unintentionally living your life — because now you have
ownership.

After taking time to read this chapter and write new agreements,
I would love to hear what you are committed to creating
(chad@forwardpartners.net).

CHAPTER 12 REFLECTION

Reflection Questions

1. Where in your life are you currently just *involved* (chicken) rather than *committed* (pig)?

2. Do your current expectations — internal or external — align with what you truly want to create for yourself, your family, and your work?

3. What old expectations or obligations do you continue to adhere to out of guilt, fear, or the need to prove, rather than out of genuine commitment?

Take Action

1. Take time this week to answer the following questions for
    yourself:

    - What do I want to create for myself?

    - What do I want to create for my family?

    - What do I want to create through my work?

2. Draft one simple agreement in each area
    that you can fully commit to (be the pig!).
    Keep your answers visible to remind
    yourself of your commitments.

3. Any time you hear the words *"should"* or *"expect"* (from
    yourself or others), pause and ask:

    - Does this align with what I've agreed to create?

    - Is it sustainable?

    - Am I willing to fully commit (chicken or pig)?

If the answers are no, either reject it or have the tough
conversation to realign.

CHAPTER 12 ENDNOTES

1. *Star Wars: Episode V — The Empire Strikes Back,* directed by Irvin Kershner (Lucasfilm Ltd., 1980).

"Shame corrodes the very part of us that believes we are capable of change."

— Dr. Brené Brown

Chapter 13

RECLAIMING JUDGMENT

I'm going to need you to leave.

In our bid to break The Burnout Cycle, judgment can convince us that change isn't possible. We believe we are broken, take on unsustainable expectations, and then judge ourselves negatively based on those expectations, confirming that we are actually not enough. In that confirmation, judgment says, "See? I told you so." That is the condemnation-style judgment that we referenced in Chapter 8, and it is *not* helpful. All it does is invite fear and shame, barrier emotions that hold us back from creation.

Judgment vs. Curiosity and Exploration

When we judge something as bad, it automatically closes doors for how we can respond. A "bad" person can only be dealt with in a limited number of ways. A "bad" result generates a limited number of responses. When we are able to withhold judgment, an infinite number of responses remain available to us. Learning to withhold condemning judgment allows us to maintain our curiosity long enough to find truth in any situation, and then take intentional action.

When we are leading through situations, our job is really that of an explorer. We need to maintain our curiosity as we explore the situation from every angle to discover truth. Anytime we jump to judge something, we are automatically closing doors of available responses. By withholding judgment — not saying it's good or bad — we can more fully examine the situation.

This is an uncomfortable idea because we are built to judge. It's how we know if something is good or bad, safe or dangerous, and it's how we stay alive.

Bear in mind that when we withhold judgment, we aren't approving of the thing. If my toddler suddenly stops in the store and begins screaming and stomping his feet, judgment can kick in. Societal norms and the disapproving looks of other shoppers prompt me to quickly judge this behavior as bad. Bad must be dealt with quickly. Since I was raised in the '80s, my move to stop it would involve threats of spanking, and if that didn't work, perhaps *an actual spanking*, right there in front of everyone.

The judgment of the action as bad shuts down curiosity and exploration. I'm not on a quest to discover why my child is suddenly screaming and stomping his feet. I'm simply putting an end to the behavior because I've judged it as bad, and I'm scared others are judging me as bad at the same time. It won't be until we return home that I discover that something had crawled into my son's shoe and bit him on the foot. Making that discovery hadn't been a possibility because my negative judgment shut down my curiosity and ability to explore. Again, I'm not saying we approve of our kid making a scene, but we don't instantly judge it as bad either. Cling tightly to curiosity. It will become a superpower.

If you are judging my example of spanking in public, this concept is working on you in real time. If you are opposed to spanking as a form of correction or punishment, you might judge my example as bad (and perhaps me a monster). With that judgment, your

brain has already begun to question everything you have read
up to this point. You might even be questioning if you want to
finish this book. After all, if I truly am a monster, what could you
possibly want to learn from me? Rest assured, dear reader, I will
have grandkids in the next few years, and I think I have evolved a
lot since my '80s upbringing and decades as a parent. My monster
days are behind me. Read on without fear.

Just like judgment of others or situations, when we judge
ourselves as bad, we close the doors of possibility. We quickly
move into prove or punish mode, to prove we aren't bad or to
punish ourselves for being bad. This is why we can struggle
to prioritize our own health — because we judge ourselves as
unworthy.

When I received my high blood pressure diagnosis, it would
have been easy to instantly judge my choices that led to that point
as bad. This would have generated more feelings of shame, and
the only way I know to handle those feelings is with poor food and
drink choices. The lack of curiosity would have led me to repeat
the same patterns again, which would have done nothing good
for my blood pressure problem. Instead, I was able to stop the
Burnout Cycle.

By withholding judgment of myself, I was able to explore with
more curiosity, to discover the "why" underneath the problem.
It was in this process that I spotted the disempowered stories
that had been driving my poor decisions. Then, I was able to seek
help, unwind those stories, and rewrite them with ones that will
continue to drive me to make *consistent* positive health choices.
This is something I had never been able to do previously because
of condemning judgments and shame.

Creating and Evaluating Success

But judgment isn't entirely bad. When I was first presenting these ideas, a woman raised her hand and asked, "But if I never use judgment, how will I know if I'm accomplishing my goals?" That's a fair question, and she is talking about evaluative judgment. This involves evaluating how we are doing, without condemning ourselves. We can focus on our results and what they say about everything ... *except our value.* The very nature of "enough-ness" is that we can't be more or less enough. If the numbers are great, we are not more enough. If they are terrible, we are not less enough. We are simply *enough.*

That being said, the eye of judgment very easily strays from our results to our identity because we are so used to the idea that our results *are* our identity. To keep judgment focused where it is actually helpful, we need a framework.

The framework I have developed is composed of what I call The Five Ingredients of Success.

1. Commitment
2. Leadership
3. Mindset
4. Effort
5. Process

These are ingredients we can use every day to create what we want and achieve our goals. These will also be our framework for evaluating our efforts, not ourselves. Notice the subtle change in language there? We are no longer judging, we are *evaluating.*

Ingredient 1: Commitment

In Chapter 11, I suggested starting each day with two questions:

1.   *What am I committed to creating today?*

2.   *What version of me needs to show up to fulfill that commitment?*

These questions will determine what you are committed to (be the pig!). True commitment to creating something will be required for it to become a reality. Problems will inevitably pop up along the way. That is where commitment will determine if you are willing to face them and create that new future, or give up and go back to doing things the chicken way.

By using evaluation instead of condemnation, you will understand where you were *truly* committed, and where you might need to go back and hold yourself accountable to recommitment. Because you are not condemning yourself, you are more likely to positively reengage with your commitment — not out of shame, but out of determination. Being the pig is a long-term process of evaluating if you've wandered off track, and then getting back on track. It's not about perfection.

Ingredient 2: Leadership

In order to live up to your commitments, you will have to lead yourself and everyone around you. In Chapter 16, we will define healthy leadership and demonstrate that if you show up as a healthy leader, you can do almost anything. If you show up as an unhealthy leader, you will always get in the way of your own success.

How well did you lead yourself and others to fulfill the commitment? Did you intentionally create the version of you that needed to show up to fulfill the commitment? Doing this is an act of leadership.

Ingredient 3: Mindset

Living up to a commitment will require the right mindset, and maintaining the right mindset requires the leadership referenced above. Leaders are always evaluating if they are on track or have wandered off course. When you spot drift (either in your team or yourself), your job is to correct it. This will often involve correcting your or your team's mindset. Your mindset is what will determine if you are able to achieve what you're after. If you commit to something, you must always maintain the mindset that you *can actually* live up to it, or you'll never be able to.

Did you let events of the day, or setbacks, knock you out of alignment with the truth? Did you allow disempowered stories to creep in and dictate how you experienced your day? These questions allow you to *evaluate* what happened to you and how well you maintained your mindset, while protecting your identity. Can you be enough and just have the wrong mindset to fulfill your commitments? Absolutely. Remember, we talked about the fact that you are never more or less enough, therefore having the wrong mindset doesn't change your identity. If you evaluate your mindset as being off target for any reason, simply recenter on the belief that you can achieve your goal.

Ingredient 4: Effort

Success will *always* require effort. Effort is the raw fuel of true success. Effort is your time, focus, energy, and resources. If you are trapped in The Burnout Cycle, it can be hard to judge how much effort is needed and where it should be directed. You will always be evaluating your effort level to ensure you are outputting the amount needed for success, but not so much that you burn out.

Did you put in the proper amount of effort today to fulfill your commitments? Did you need more or less effort? Are you defaulting to just throwing maximum effort at a problem as a brute-force solution, or are you pausing long enough to decide how to apply the right amount of effort?

Ingredient 5: Process

Proper processes funnel and focus your effort so that you can achieve the outcomes you are after. How well did you adhere to the process today?

Did you go to the gym with a focused plan, or just show up and randomly use machines? Did you follow your sales steps to the letter, or get lazy and ignore them? Well-defined processes will give you the most efficient path to achievement.

Evaluating Results

When evaluating your (or someone else's) results, work down through The Five Ingredients of Success to see how well you lived up to each, or where you went off track. If the results didn't meet the goal, then this exercise will help you discover the source of the problem. Use the following questions to evaluate.

Did you fully commit to the goals?

Did you intentionally lead yourself and those around you?

Did you maintain the right mindset?

Did you put in the proper amount of effort?

Did you properly follow the processes everyone agreed to?

The goal of using evaluation is to reclaim judgment and make it productive. When we use judgment in a condemning way, it creates fear and shame, which is what we're used to. When we evaluate results, we can process them — either good or bad — while still affirming that *we are enough.*

Let's take a salesman as an example. Let's pretend this guy's name is … I don't know, I'm just pulling this name out of the air … *Carl.* Let's say Carl woke up and made a commitment to sell three TVs by the end of the day. He intentionally created the version of himself that is capable of selling three TVs by the end of the day. He created a winning mindset that would power him to success. He quickly sold one TV, but around midday, an unhappy customer showed up and gave him a really hard time. This made Carl feel fear and shame, and instead of resetting his mindset, he took a long lunch, spent most of the afternoon distractedly scrolling through Instagram, and sold no more TVs. At the end of the day, you, as Carl's manager, have to go over his results.

What does condemnation look like when we judge?

"Hey, Carl, you put three TVs on the board as your goal, but you only sold one. You suck!"

"Hey, Carl, you put three TVs on the board as your goal, but you only sold one. What the hell?"

"Hey, Carl, you put three TVs on the board as your goal, but you only sold one. Loser."

While you may not use those words, any judgment that generates shame will *feel* like you are using these words. Judging someone's results, and protecting that person from fear and shame, takes far more empathy, grace, and finesse. It's not just your words, but also your tone and facial expressions, that communicate. So how can you give Carl the best chance at success tomorrow? By using evaluation instead of condemnation.

"Hey, Carl, you put three TVs on the board as your goal, but you only sold one. You should be proud of that one. Let's break down what happened with the rest. Did you fully commit to selling three TVs today?"

Carl thinks about it for a moment, then says, "I thought I had. I was up early and I did the work to remind myself that I'm enough and decide how I needed to show up in order to sell those TVs."

"Okay, so it sounds like you committed and then led yourself well. That's the first two ingredients. What about mindset? Did you create the right mindset to allow yourself to achieve your goal?"

"I did! I did all the work to create the right mindset first thing this morning. I *believed* today was going to be my day, and I created a mindset of service to my customers, just like you taught me."

"That's great. Did you maintain it throughout the day?"

"Yeah, I ... wait, no, I guess I didn't. That customer that came in right before lunch ..."

"That guy who was being a jackass?"

"Yeah, he really pissed me off. I guess he got under my skin. I *never* got my mindset back on track after that."

"I think we figured it out. What happened to your effort and processes after that?"

"Clearly nothing good. I only sold one TV. All my effort went into scrolling on Instagram."

"Which doesn't really pay the bills, does it?"

"Not even a little. Because there was no effort, there wasn't a reason to really follow processes. I stopped greeting customers within thirty seconds of entering the store. I waited for them to come to me."

"Which we know is not the best way to connect with a customer."

"I know."

"So what is your focus going to be tomorrow?"

"Keeping my mindset squared all day."

"If you have any trouble with that, just ask for help. I'm here for you. We all have days like today. I'm proud of you, and you should be proud of yourself for creating a plan for tomorrow. I'll see you then."

What is the goal? The goal is for Carl to understand his results, and what led to them, in a way that gives him the *best* chance at success tomorrow. If you, as his leader, can withhold negative judgment, then you can hold onto the curiosity to help him evaluate the situation. The default is to shame people into submission, but shame *never* leads to consistent long-term results, and it does damage along the way. If Carl leaves feeling shame, he is going to have a bad evening. Then, he'll show up the next day haunted by shame, and he is unlikely to use The Five Ingredients to create success. If he shows up feeling encouraged and supported, he is *more* likely to consider commitment, leadership, mindset, effort, and process.

You might be thinking, "Well, that sounds *weak!*"

I know, I get it. I'm a Gen X kid raised by Boomers. I know *all* about shame as a motivator. But the fact is, we've learned a lot over the past few decades about how humans work. And it turns out that support, belief, and, dare I say, love, are far better motivators than fear and shame.

As a leader, one of your most important jobs is to pull fear and shame out of the system. That's true for yourself and for the people you lead. Using evaluation for understanding will reveal the path to achieving your goals. Carl needs to keep his mindset on track tomorrow, and now you know to check in with him and see how he's doing.

Is there eventually a line where Carl is no longer employable? Sure. And you should communicate openly about that fact, while also giving him the resources and leadership to succeed. And if you ever have to let Carl go (*poor, Carl*), it should never be a surprise. But Carl's *best* chance to succeed is with the confidence that comes from believing that he is enough as a human being, even if his results are lacking. His *best* chance is if you help him learn to use evaluation to be curious instead of condemning. All the while, reassuring him of the truth — that he is whole, complete, and nothing is wrong with him. That version of him can *create* success.

The same is true for you.

CHAPTER 13 REFLECTION

Reflection Questions

1. Where in your life do you habitually judge yourself or others, rather than exploring and understanding the situation?

2. When you experience negative results, do you default to shame or curiosity? How might shifting to curiosity change your response?

3. How could focusing on evaluation (commitment, leadership, mindset, effort, process) instead of condemnation improve your personal or professional outcomes?

Take Action

1. When you notice judgment arising (in yourself or toward others), pause and ask:

    *   What's the story behind this behavior or result?

    *   What can I learn by exploring it instead of judging it?

    *   How could I respond in a way that preserves options and energy? Practice turning automatic judgment into intentional exploration.

2. At the end of each day, pick one result or situation where you might have judged yourself. Instead of saying "I failed" or "I'm bad," work through The Five Ingredients of Success:

    *   Commitment: Did I fully commit?

    *   Leadership: Did I lead myself and others well?

    *   Mindset: Did I maintain a productive mindset?

    *   Effort: Did I give the right amount of time, focus, energy, and resources?

    *   Process: Did I follow the right processes?

Note which ingredient you need to use more of tomorrow. Avoid tying results to your worth.

"Momentum begets momentum, and the best way to start is to start."

— Gil Penchina
angel investor, and former CEO of Wikia, Inc.

Chapter 14

PUTTING IT ALL TOGETHER: THE MOMENTUM CYCLE

THE MOMENTUM CYCLE

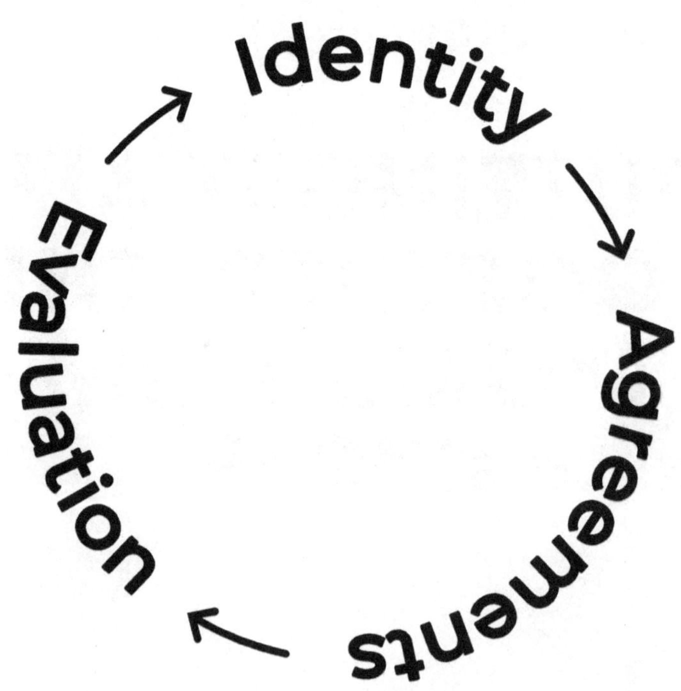

The three elements of identity, expectations, and judgments have conspired to keep you trapped in The Burnout Cycle for much of your life. This means that wrestling with burnout has most likely become normal for you. By reclaiming all three elements, you can replace The Burnout Cycle with The Momentum Cycle.

You can own an identity that's aligned with the truth that you are enough. You can write agreements about *what* you want to create and *how* you will create it. You can evaluate any expectations presented to you and decide if you will take them on or not, based on how well they align with your short- and long-term agreements. You can also regularly use evaluation to assess how well you are living up to your commitments, discover obstacles, and decide on next steps.

As you intentionally use these three elements to create the life you want, you will be engaging in The Momentum Cycle. The more you show up as your best self, and achieve success with your agreements, the more momentum you will build toward an ever brighter future. You will begin to envision new levels of growth and possibility that The Burnout Cycle has been robbing you of all this time.

Welcome to Your New Job

Your primary job is to lead yourself and to maintain The Momentum Cycle in your life. You will find that when you show up as your most authentic self, the world around you will start to change because you are actually able to create the outcomes you want. Does this mean everything in life will fall into place like a red carpet of success rolling out before you? Absolutely not.

Maintaining The Momentum Cycle takes consistent work — it requires you to *lead*. This act of leadership, first of yourself and then of others, is what will allow you to create new outcomes. Maintaining alignment with the truth of your identity and value will also help you unlock other people's ability to see *their* true identity and value. You've encountered leaders with this ability before. They are the elementary school teachers you still remember because they had such a big impact on you. They are the bosses who saw your true potential and gave you an opportunity before anyone else would. They are the friends who steadfastly led you through the biggest challenges of your life by reminding you that you were strong enough to take action.

When your life is dictated by The Momentum Cycle, you can be that leader for everyone around you. Regardless of title or rank, you will *lead* everyone you come into contact with. That is true positive impact. And when you lead this way, free of The Burnout Cycle, you can achieve Sustainable Impact — the multiplied impact of chasing your purpose with patience and healthy rhythms.

Erwin McManus, in his book *Mind Shift: It Doesn't Take a Genius to Think Like One*, says, "May the ever-expanding universe inside you become your gift to the world. May everyone who crosses your path be blessed by the person you have become and the world you have created. May you always be a beacon pointing to the noble and honorable and best of humanity. With every breath, may you be a light in dark places, and proof of life to those holding on with a silent desperation. May your life be an inspiration to all dreamers yet to come."[1]

This is what is possible when we can maintain The Momentum Cycle because it is our most authentic selves leading our most authentic lives. My prayer every day is that I can embody this ideal by showing up as ... *me*.

Practical Action

So how do we do that? It's one thing to be excited about an idea, but to do it and even sustain it for years requires *practical action*. View this next section as a checklist to maintain The Momentum Cycle. As simple as the following actions are, like going to the gym and making wise food choices, repeating them consistently will lead to life-changing results. And the beauty is — these actions are available to *everyone*.

I don't care how rich or poor you are.

I don't care what race or religion you are.

I don't care how burned out you are.

There is *nothing* stopping you from taking the following actions to win the battle against burnout.

Morning Routine - Creation Practices

The morning is the best time to begin the work. You are responsible for creating the version of you that will face all the challenges stacked against you that day. Begin with the two questions we've discussed previously:

1.   *What am I committed to creating today?*

2.   *What version of me needs to show up to fulfill that
     commitment?*

If you haven't already, write down your answers. Get specific.
What are you committed to creating? Do you want to sell a certain
number of products? Are you committed to getting your kids out
the door without losing your cool? Are you committed to finally
having a difficult conversation with your coworker? This morning,
my commitment was to write two chapters of this book, including
these words right here.

What version of you needs to show up to fulfill that
commitment? Here's a breakdown:

> **Commitment:** I *will* sell five cars today.
> **Being:** I need to *be* energy, optimism,
> connection, communication, determination.
> **Action:** Follow up with leads from yesterday.
> Stay on process. Hustle.

> **Commitment:** I *will* get my kids out the door
> without losing my cool.
> **Being:** I need to *be* patience, consistency,
> determination, love, and positivity.
> **Action:** Stretch and meditate. Have my coffee.
> Put on body armor.

> **Commitment:** I *will* have a difficult
> conversation with my coworker today.
> **Being:** I need to *be* courage, empathy,
> determination, grace, curiosity, and clarity.
> **Action:** Pray. Go for a walk ahead of time. Have
> the conversation.

> **Commitment:** I *will* write two chapters of this book today.
> **Being:** I need to *be* focus, creativity, energy, clarity, and insight.
> **Action:** Have my coffee and water. Sit down at the keyboard. Tap, tap, tapity, tap.

Any day that you don't intentionally decide what you are committed to creating is a day that you let circumstance, challenges, and other people decide for you. That will always be a path to burnout.

Now that you know what version of you is needed to fulfill your commitments, get to work. If you are looking for music for this part of the process, I highly recommend the score from *Top Gun: Maverick* by Hans Zimmer. Let's start by zeroing out any disempowered programming that might have snuck in yesterday.

Take a deep breath in, then exhale and say out loud, "I am whole, complete, and there is nothing wrong with me. I am enough."

Repeat it again. "I am whole, complete, and there is nothing wrong with me. I am enough."

Repeat it as many times as necessary to overcome The Bullshit Response. Repeat it until you feel a sense of peace or excitement, or a smile comes to your face. Those are signs you are aligned with the truth of who you are and your internal computer has reset. Now it's time to add some new code based on the "Being" list you made for the day.

I Am:

- *Focus*
- *Creativity*
- *Energy*
- *Clarity*
- *Insight*

Speak your entire list out loud, plus any other aspects of yourself that you know would be helpful for the day. Now you have set your internal programming.

The Plan

Once you have your set of commitments, and have done your creation practices, it's time to create a plan for the day using The Five Ingredients for Success. Your commitments for the day are the first ingredient for success. Now, work through the other four:

How do you need to lead yourself and others to fulfill those commitments?

What mindset is going to allow you to succeed?

How much effort do you need to put in?

What processes will help you succeed?

Quickly jot down answers to these questions, and you'll have a simple framework to evaluate how well you are living up to your commitments and whether adjustments are needed.

Green Light Habits

Once you have done the hard work of commitment, creation, and planning, now it's time to layer on some Green Light Habits. Green Light Habits is a concept I developed years ago to help myself stay on track. Since then, we've been deploying it to help people determine the best actions they can take for themselves throughout the day.

At its core, the concept of Green Light Habits is simply a list of healthy choices. From the moment you wake up, to the moment you go to bed, what are the *healthy* choices you know you should make for yourself? That list becomes a guide to help you stay on track throughout a day.

I use my list of Green Light Habits not only to guide myself through the day, but also to evaluate my performance at the end of the week. I pull up my list each weekend, and highlight in green any habits that I observed regularly. Habits I tried, but wasn't very consistent with, will get a yellow highlight. Habits that I didn't really do at all will get a red. Inevitably, weeks that I judge as bad are weeks that coincide with a lot of red and yellow on my worksheet. And weeks that I judge as good, happen to be weeks where I have a lot of green and almost no red.

In doing this, I can see visually that my experience of a week largely comes down to how consistently I observed healthy habits. Every week has its challenges, but my experience of the week comes down to my choices. When I choose to show up as a healthy leader, I face those challenges in a healthy way. The opposite is true when I show up in an unhealthy way.

Here's an example of a basic Green Light Habits list:
- Get up early
- Meditate and stretch
- Pray about the day
- Eat a high-protein breakfast (with coffee!)
- Get to work fifteen minutes early
- Eat salad for lunch
- Go for an afternoon walk
- Drink water throughout the day
- Dinner before 7:00 p.m.
- Bed by 10:00 p.m.

Everyone's Green Light Habits list will look slightly different. (What are you eating or drinking in the morning? Are you taking time for reflection and creation? Are you moving your body in any way, from stretching to a full workout?) Whatever your list looks like, your items will be the choices that will help you win the battle against burnout. But beware, The Burnout Cycle will often prevent you from making these choices (or at least give you an excuse not to).

The morning will be the most difficult time to invest in yourself for many people (parents of young kids, in particular). I've also found that not being intentional the night before, particularly with what you consume before bed and when you go to bed, have a real effect on what your morning looks like. Unfortunately, just because the morning is a challenge for you, doesn't change the fact that it is the *most vital* point of creation in your entire day. Your actions each morning will determine how the rest of the day goes.

Of course, you don't want to fall into The Perfection Trap we discussed in Chapter 7. My morning routine is rarely *perfect*. However, I don't let that stop me from making intentional choices. I may not be able to do everything I would like to invest in myself, but I can do *something*.

Pause to Check In

It's time to dive into your day. Throughout this day, you are going to have a lot thrown at you. Stress, challenges, and inevitably your Carl will conspire to wreck your carefully laid plans. Some of these things will cause you to question your identity and value. It will sometimes knock you out of alignment with the truth of who you are. Your job is to maintain that alignment. Check in with yourself throughout the day to determine if you are still aligned or not. Refer back to the questions we discussed in Chapter 6 to see if you are aligned with truth:

Do I feel the need to prove anything right now?

Do I feel the need to punish myself for something?

If the answer to either question is yes, it's a sign you have been knocked out of alignment and it's worth realigning. Look for any disempowered stories in your answers, and do the work to unwind and rewrite any that you discover. Then go back to your creation practices, reminding yourself what you are committed to and who you need to be today. Remind yourself of the truth, "I am whole, complete, and there is nothing wrong with me. I am enough." These check-ins should happen regularly throughout the day, even if you are doing well.

I've found that there are natural points in the day when a pause to check in can happen easily. I try to pause to check in at three specific points:

1. When I am entering a meeting
2. When I encounter something very stressful
3. When I am sitting down to do focused or important work

At each of these points, a quick pause and reflection will reveal any misalignment. This is also a great time to pull out your list of Green Light Habits. What's the next healthy choice you can make for yourself? Go refill your water bottle, choose a healthy lunch, or go for a quick walk?

Now get back out there and keep fighting.

Evaluation

When you do your check-ins, it can also be a good time to quickly run down The Five Ingredients chain and see how well you are creating success. Are you following your processes, putting in the proper effort, maintaining your mindset, and leading yourself and others? How well are you living up to your commitments for the day?

If the evaluation reveals that you are off track in any area, you can refocus and take action to get back on track. It's also good to do a final evaluation at the end of the day.

Intentionality

All of this is the intentionality required to win the battle against burnout. If burnout is acting with intention to harm you, then you must apply more intention to combat it. By observing these practices, you are ensuring that you are in control of all of your choices. You are not letting stress, fear, shame, or burnout choose for you.

You can unintentionally create something great, but you can't unintentionally *sustain* something great. You could unintentionally stumble into a low-stress day filled with peace and success. However, there are too many forces working against you to be able to unintentionally repeat those days long-term. You have the power of choice. Use it.

Wash, Rinse, Repeat

Maintaining The Momentum Cycle is about maintaining your *freedom*. Free from the need to prove anything, free from unsustainable expectations, and free from condemning judgments, you can readily choose how you want to live your life. You can center on the truth of your identity, create agreements, and evaluate your progress. Maintaining this cycle isn't complex, and the results can be revolutionary.

I know when I wake up each morning, my most important work is to engage and maintain The Momentum Cycle so I can continue to positively impact the people around me.

This is what a life of service to others looks like.

This is what a life of *purpose* looks like.

This is what leadership looks like.

CHAPTER 14 REFLECTION

Reflection Questions

1. How often do you let circumstance, challenges, or other people dictate your day instead of being directed by your own commitments?

2. Which Green Light Habits would have the biggest positive effect on how you show up?

3. When you feel out of alignment, what disempowered stories are you telling yourself that need to be unwound?

Take Action

1. Embrace morning creation practices by taking time to write down your plan. Start with these two questions each morning:

   What am I committed to creating today?

   What version of me needs to show up to fulfill that commitment?

   - Write a success plan using the Five Ingredients for Success.

   - Use Green Light Habits to intentionally invest in your health.

CHAPTER 14 ENDNOTES

1. Erwin McManus, *Mind Shift: It Doesn't Take a Genius to Think Like One* (Convergent Books, 2023), 134.

"The greatest enemy of the truth is very often not the lie, deliberate contrived, and dishonest, but the myth, persistent, persuasive, and unrealistic."

— Michael Jordan

Chapter 15

DESTROYING MYTHS

Myths

Throughout the course of this work, we've come across many common myths about our identities, work, rest, and value. I have believed and lived by many of these myths. These are all disempowered stories and will contribute to The Burnout Cycle instead of The Momentum Cycle.

As you look at the following pages, I want you to think about the number of times you have heard, believed, or said these stories. Let's take the time to unwind each of these and write an empowered story we can use any time the myths pop up. You might also recognize other myths that are trapping you in burnout.

Myth - Rest must be earned. Once I've done "enough," I can rest.

Payoff:

- I don't have to learn to rest (relieved of responsibility).

- I can just put my head down and work (relieved of responsibility).

Cost:

- I never learn to rest.

- I burn out.

- The quality of my work suffers.

- The quality of my relationships suffer.

- My health suffers.

- I die.

Empowered Story - Rest comes before productivity, not productivity before rest.

Myth - Rest is not productive. It is lazy.

Payoff:

- When I don't rest, I'm productive (feel superior).

- I'm not a lazy person (feel superior).

- Productivity is more important than rest (feel superior).

- I don't have to learn to rest (relieved of responsibility).

Cost:

- I never learn to rest.

- I burn out.

- The quality of my work suffers.

- The quality of my relationships suffer.

- My health suffers.

- I die. (This seems familiar.)

Empowered Story - I am designed to rest and it is the key to creating success.

Myth - My value is based on how productive I am.

Payoff:

- If I check off a lot of tasks, I feel valuable (feel superior).

- A lack of productivity confirms my feelings of being broken (relieved of responsibility).

- All I'm required to focus on is doing work (relieved of responsibility).

Cost:

- I'm trapped in a loop of never feeling productive enough.

- My only move is to just work harder.

- I burn out.

- The quality of my work suffers.

- The quality of my relationships suffer.

- My health suffers.

- I die. (That old story again.)

Empowered Story - I am enough, no matter how productive I am. I am whole, complete, and there is nothing wrong with me.

Myth - I should have accomplished X thing by Y date. (Insert your own X and Y.)

Payoff:

- Because I didn't meet that arbitrary deadline, I can give up (relieved of responsibility).

- Missing the deadline confirms my feelings of being broken (relieved of responsibility).

Cost:

- I approach every day with a feeling of being behind.

- I take on unsustainable expectations to try to catch up.

- I burn out.

- The quality of my work suffers.

- The quality of my relationships suffer.

- My health suffers.

- I should myself to death.

Empowered Story - I am living my story and am exactly where I'm supposed to be on the journey.

To quote Gandalf in *The Lord of the Rings: The Fellowship of the Ring,* "A wizard is never late. Nor is he early. He arrives precisely when he means to." [1]

Myth - Asking for help is a weakness.

Payoff:

- I never ask for help because I'm strong (feel superior).
- I'm strong, so I never need to ask for help (relieved of responsibility).

Cost:

- I feel the need to overcome every obstacle alone.
- I lose the insight that outside help can bring.
- I repeat the same patterns over and over.
- I burn out.
- The quality of my work suffers.
- The quality of my relationships suffer.
- My health suffers.
- (You guessed it.) Dead.

Empowered Story - Asking for help demonstrates inner-strength and confidence to those around me.

Myth - If I show vulnerability, people will not follow me.

Payoff:

- I am a great leader because I am never vulnerable (feel superior).
- I never have to learn to be vulnerable (relieved of responsibility).

Cost:

- My people never fully trust me.
- I can never be vulnerable, which means I can never ask for help.
- I remain trapped in loneliness.
- I burn out.
- The quality of my work suffers.
- The quality of my relationships suffer.
- My health suffers.
- I live a long, healthy life. (Just kidding. I die.)

Empowered Story - Healthy vulnerability is a courageous act of service and leadership.

Myth - I'll be happy when I get my next X. (Solve for X.)

Payoff:

- All I have to do is focus on what's next (relieved of responsibility to focus on today).

- Focusing on what's next is always exciting (feel excited without actually doing anything).

Cost:

- By not focusing on today, I never create the tomorrow I want.

- I never feel happy because I can't get to X.

- I burn out.

- The quality of my work suffers.

- The quality of my relationships suffer.

- My health suffers.

- (Imagine a skull and crossbones emoji here.)

Empowered Story - I will experience joy by showing up as my authentic self, being present, and serving those around me.

CHAPTER 15 REFLECTION

Reflection Questions

1. Which of the myths do you currently recognize in your life?

2. Which empowered story resonates most strongly with you, and how can you apply it today?

Are there recurring patterns in your life where believing these myths has led to burnout or frustration?

....

....

....

....

....

....

....

Take Action

Identify Your Myths

- Write down the top three to five myths you believe most strongly.

- Note how they have influenced your behavior, decisions, and energy.

- Unwind each one and rewrite each as an empowered story.

CHAPTER 15 ENDNOTES

1. *The Lord of the Rings: The Fellowship of the Ring,* directed by Peter Jackson (New Line Cinema, 2001).

Part 4

MOVING FORWARD

"Do not follow
where the path
may lead. Go
instead where
there is no path
and leave a trail."

— Ralph Waldo Emerson

Chapter 16

WINNING THE BATTLE

Much like we unwind disempowered stories and replace them with empowered stories, we need to replace a disempowered image — the image of a person pushing a boulder up the hill to create success. For too long, this image has ensnared us. Our fear is that if we don't have that weight to push against, what will drive us? The problem is, the weight is made up of The Burnout Cycle and it keeps us trapped and suffering in The Burnout Curve.

It is not a picture of success. It is a picture of burnout.

Therefore, we will replace it with this empowered picture: Instead of one person pushing a boulder up a hill, picture a group of leaders who have decided to climb together. No one is pushing a boulder up the mountain. In fact, there are no boulders in sight. It is simply a team, fully equipped for the climb, supporting one another as they move forward together. They have decided that the journey up the mountain is one they will give themselves to completely. They have decided the best way to do this is as a thriving team.

"But I don't have a team," I hear you say. Later in this chapter, we'll discuss how to make sure you have your team properly built out by recruiting your own Circle of Support. But first, let's explore the definition of "healthy leadership" because a thriving team requires healthy leaders.

———

Healthy leaders are spiritually, emotionally, and physically oriented toward health.

———

Orientation

You'll notice the definition of healthy leadership doesn't say anything about being at the peak of spiritual, emotional, and physical health. This means that we *all* have the opportunity to be healthy leaders.

As I write this, I'm making good progress on losing weight, but I'm still at least thirty pounds overweight. Despite that fact, I got up this morning and made an incredibly healthy breakfast and went for a walk. These two actions served to orient me toward health.

If you go back and look at the Green Light Habits, you'll note that each of those choices should orient you toward health in one or more of the three categories: spiritual, emotional, and physical. If orientation toward health, not perfection, is the goal, then we are always one intentional action away from reorienting toward health. Healthy leadership comes from a series of healthy choices followed by healthy actions. It's not about perfection, just intentional orientation.

Spiritually Healthy

Are you seeing purpose and impact in your daily life and leadership?

Spiritual health is about a connection to the big picture. Being spiritually healthy gives rise to an awareness of our place in a larger narrative; it allows us to aspire to make an impact beyond what we would otherwise be capable of. The determination to chase a larger purpose can give us the discipline necessary to lead ourselves well. The impact yielded by chasing purpose will provide the inspiration and energy that is required when the battle becomes difficult.

Spiritual practices lead to an understanding that we are not the center of the universe. We are part of a larger story, and our purpose is found in service to others. Every action we take is like dropping a pebble into the water. There will be ripples of impact that flow outward. When we are spiritually healthy, we realize that every word and action has the potential for tremendous impact on others; therefore, we are *intentional* with every word and action. The larger the world we see, the larger the positive impact we can have.

When we are spiritually unhealthy, our world becomes very small — it becomes all about *us*. We lose sight of purpose and impact. We begin to elevate things to a level of importance that they should not hold. We begin to obsess over what's next, as though that next promotion, car, phone, watch, or trip will be *ultimately* satisfying. Life becomes a chase for the next *thing* rather than about chasing purpose and impact. We *need* the next thing because the last thing wasn't as satisfying as we thought, and now we need *more*. Life becomes very small indeed. It also sounds a lot like burnout.

Everyone's spiritual practices look different. For many, it will involve faith or religious practices. Worship and fellowship are reminders of a person's place in the universe and that we aren't meant to live life alone. One of the most spiritual things I do is go for a walk in the park on a Saturday morning. Seeing how big the bright, blue sky is, hearing the birds, and seeing the trees sway in the wind remind me that life happens without me. My impact can and will be great, but the world is so much bigger than just me.

Whatever your spiritual practices are, they should connect you to the bigger picture and motivate you to purpose and service.

Emotionally Healthy

Have you been communicating and leading with empathy and grace?

As we lead, if we find ourselves constantly frustrated and lacking empathy or grace, it's a sign we are emotionally tired. When we are struggling emotionally, empathy and grace are the first two things to go out the window. We become very inwardly focused when we are in a tough place. Everything is viewed through the lens of how it affects us, instead of how it affects others. An outward focus requires emotional health.

Regarding empathy, some people have the actual gift of feeling other people's feelings. Some of us don't even want to feel our *own* feelings, much less someone else's. However, *all of us* can pause and ask the question, "How will this affect the person on the other side of the table?" Just by asking the question, we are taking a step toward empathy. We are attempting to understand how someone will experience something. Even if we pull emotion out of it, logically working through this question is still an act of empathy. Healthy leaders will not only consider the other person's experience, we will also modify how we approach something in order to give that person the best possible experience.

And when I talk about grace, I don't mean *infinite* grace. I simply mean flexibility. In leadership, there are times when we can be flexible, and we should be flexible. There are also times when flexibility is no longer possible. Our job is to discern which is which, and that requires emotional health to do well. We are leading people, and, as we established in a previous chapter, people are insanely complex. The more flexible we can be, the more we create space for that complexity to exist.

Physically Healthy

Are you valuing and modeling good rest and healthy habits?

In a world of twenty-four seven hustle, it is hard to step back and truly value rest and good physical habits. As leaders, however, it is our job to not only employ those rhythms for our own good, but to lead our teams down the same path.

The goal of this entire book is to put you in a place where you can value yourself enough to prioritize intentional rest as an investment in your success. You and I have struggled with this for so long, and we are not alone. Our teams struggle right alongside us.

Much like our children, the people we lead will follow what we model more than what we say. It is not enough to say we want *them* to rest, we have to lead the way by showing them how. We have to learn to embrace healthy rhythms, truly disconnect from work, and intentionally create success.

We also have to model healthy habits beyond just rest. As I have gone on my health journey, I have been modeling better eating and exercise habits for my team. I've noticed they have begun to take on some of those same habits. We are now on a healthier journey together because I am leading the way.

If your responsibility is ensuring that The Burnout Curve is shallow for you and your team, then modeling physical health will be one of the biggest factors in your success.

Once we engage The Momentum Cycle and show up as healthy leaders, we can then deploy the other three tools needed to win the battle against burnout: self-awareness, purpose, and rhythms.

Embracing Self-Awareness

Self-awareness is an understanding of ourselves — not just who we are, but how we are navigating leadership, and how we are being experienced by the people around us. When we are healthy, we have the ability to transform the world for the better — to achieve heroic levels of leadership. When we don't *intentionally choose* to show up as a healthy leader, we are unintentionally choosing average ... or worse. At average levels, we are unintentionally doing damage to the people around us. At unhealthy levels, we are looking to burn it all to the ground. Failing to choose health is an abdication of our most important responsibility as leaders — to care for the people we have influence over.

The self-awareness needed to have a real-time understanding of how we are showing up requires cultivation. Through regular self-reflection exercises, we will be able to build the muscles of self-awareness. This will enable us to recognize when we are struggling, misaligned from the truth of our identity, or operating with a disempowered story. We can then intentionally take action to create a healthier version of ourselves.

To facilitate regular self-reflection exercises, we have created an entirely free online course. You can sign up yourself and your team for free at: https://www.forwardpartners.net/reflect.

The exercise consists of four simple reflection questions, a leadership health rating system, and a plan for next steps. All-in, it takes about ten minutes to fill out the worksheet. The questions, while simple, will generate deep insight and conversation. It's good to consider your last week when reflecting on these questions:

1. What has been your biggest win?
2. What has been your biggest challenge?
3. Who have you impacted positively?
4. Who has positively impacted you?

Using this course as a guide, you can practice regular self-reflection. And if you have a team, you can have deep conversations about how everyone is really doing. This will reveal valuable insights and next steps on your journey. Over time, these rhythms will build your self-awareness to a real-time level — where you are aware in the moment, rather than just on reflection. I work through this exercise every week, always finding insight in my reflection, and building my self-awareness. Healthy leaders are self-aware leaders.

Living with Purpose on Purpose

Much like self-awareness, purpose can seem soft and squishy, unable to truly impact our day-to-day leadership. The reality is that our purpose is as practical as a hammer. It provides a new bar for success. It gives us a sense of meaning and a North Star to guide our lives. It provides energy and motivation. It defines the "why" of our existence.

All humans have a deep need to be a part of something larger than themselves — a need to know that we matter. Our purpose simply defines how we are meant to make a difference in the world.

Burnout would like us focused on an infinite sea of tasks so that we will lose sight of the big picture. The big picture (available to us when we are oriented toward spiritual health) shows us that we are designed to have a huge impact on everyone we encounter.

Being driven by that purpose will enable us to do the hard work — hard work, like asking for help, going to therapy, and taking time off. That's *the work*, and we're going to struggle to do it if we aren't driven by a deep and abiding purpose.

As we live out our purpose and see the positive impact on others, it will become energizing. We'll begin to look for more opportunities to have a positive impact. In fact, it might become so motivating that we'll need the rhythms of the next section to serve as a throttle. Burnout doesn't just happen when we chase unhealthy things. It will often take over when we chase *good* things — like impact — but without boundaries or healthy rhythms.

Honoring Rhythms

Burnout has a rhythm. It shows up each morning to whisper lies in our ears, kickstarting The Burnout Cycle, and robbing us of our potential impact. We've learned the rhythms of our enemy and how to counter those efforts. We are designed to observe certain rhythms of our own. In this section, we'll briefly look at the three rhythms we are designed to honor. Establishing these rhythms, and combining them with self-awareness and purpose, will give us the tools necessary to win the battle against burnout.

Rhythms of Connection — Building Your Circle of Support

Staying trapped in The Burnout Cycle often happens because we refuse to ask for help, determined to go it alone as proof of our strength. However, as humans, we are designed to *need* connection with other people. Connection with our Circle of Support will become an important rhythm to help us win the battle against Burnout. It won't take long to realize that a Circle filled with intentional relationships will take serious work. Begin by identifying people you need in three categories: professional help, mentors, and fellow leaders.

Professional Help

Every leader should have some combination of a coach, therapist, doctor, physical trainer, or spiritual director. Sometimes, all five. (And yes, that includes you.) Doctors and physical trainers are pretty self-explanatory. Therapists, coaches, and spiritual directors are foreign concepts for a lot of us.

A coach is there to provide insight and strategies to help us get better at something. Most coaching relationships are limited in nature. We are usually trying to develop a specific skill or area of our life. Once that is accomplished, it's time to move on to the next area. That might involve the same coach, but it could also involve a new one.

A therapist is there to help us as we examine ourselves, giving us tools to deal with the past trauma that will prevent us from accomplishing the things we want. Despite living in a world that seems more open to the idea of therapy, there is still a stigma that will stop many people from pursuing healing through this route. It is still often seen as the road only taken by crazy people, as if clear proof that there is something deeply wrong with them.

I'm here to tell you, *we all need therapy.* All of us, no matter our background, have experienced trauma. Our bodies, minds, and souls bear the scars of trauma. None of us escape unscathed. And the bad part is, if we don't do something about it, the people around us will begin to bear the scars of our trauma as well. Ensuring that past trauma doesn't dictate your future is one of the strongest and most courageous things you will ever do.

A spiritual director helps us wrestle with the bigger questions in life. If we have ever experienced trauma involving religion or faith, it's good to have an outside perspective to guide us on that journey. Many people are content to throw their hands up and give up on the idea of a healthy spiritual life. Spiritual health, however, is a key component of being a healthy leader. Spiritual directors can ensure we have someone to support us as we start to untangle past hurts and establish healthy spiritual practices.

All of these connections are vital in that they are professional relationships — we are *paying* them for their service. This can help us open up with a vulnerability that we may struggle to show to others. Investing in our growth financially can be painful, but it is the single most important investment you will ever make. My journey to align with the truth of who I am did not really begin until I sought professional help.

Mentors

We should seek out leaders who are ahead of us on the journey. Great mentors will have built what we want to build, or have endured what we must endure. Having a relationship with a mentor will help us find strategies and hope on our difficult journey. These connections also give the mentor a chance to share their hard-fought truths, which in turn, gives meaning to their struggles.

Over time, we might outgrow our mentor, meaning we have tapped into all their knowledge and are now facing challenges that are beyond their experience. Then it is time to find our next mentor, someone who's ahead of us, and begin a new relationship.

When I begin to look for a new mentor, I write a short description of what they have built and how they operate. I then send that description out to everyone I can think of and ask them to introduce me to that person. This method has never failed me, and has always led to a life-changing mentorship.

Fellow Leaders (Peers and Friends)

It is good to have a group of leaders who are at a similar place as we are on the journey. We will be able to share similar experiences and help in real time as we each wrestle with challenges. This portion of our Circle of Support is probably the most enduring. While we will outgrow coaches and mentors, this group can grow *together*.

In this group, we'll find a deep understanding because our peers and friends are usually right alongside us, in the same season of life. They provide support to go along with the tools and wisdom we receive from the other two parts of our Circle.

Like all the other parts of our Circle, we will have to intentionally create connections with fellow leaders. Great friends will not magically fall into our lap. Finding and deepening relationships takes work. One of my current focuses is on being a better friend. I have a small group of friends with whom I'm committed to being proactive. I'm just beginning to get intentional about this, but I'm already finding it to be incredibly rewarding work. Our world seems to be moving faster and faster, the demands on our time increasing. It's on us to create intentional space to slow down and connect deeply with others.

Rhythms of Creation — Green Light Habits

In Chapter 14, we covered creation practices and Green Light Habits. Remember, if we are not regularly embracing commitment, choosing how we are going to show up, and taking intentional action, we are giving up our ability to create a thriving future. That surrender is so sad because it is so unintentional.

We know the future that burnout has in store for us (every disempowered story eventually ends how?), and the only way to fix that is to embrace regular rhythms of creation.

Rhythms of Restoration — Intentional Rest Planning

We are designed to need certain rhythms of rest. When we intentionally honor those rhythms, we are putting ourselves in the best position to rest. With each of the rhythms we are about to explore, bear in mind one distinction: When we say rest, we mean *restoration*. Most people think of rest as an inactive state; however, true restoration comes from restorative *action*. We are intentionally choosing activities that bring life back to our souls.

Restoration looks different for everyone. For introverts like me, it involves reading books (with a good scotch in hand) or taking a solo walk in the park. For extroverts, it might be attending a concert, baseball game, or friend's birthday party. It's all about identifying things that energize us rather than draining us. Whatever we choose for rest, the point is to intentionally *choose something*, and to do it according to certain rhythms.

Create intentional plans for the following rhythms:

Daily

If you are finishing each day tired but fulfilled, practicing good sleep habits will restore you, ensuring you can have an impact again the next day. However, the daily practice of rest goes well beyond just sleep. Each evening, it's good to take intentional action and find small ways to fill your cup back up. Wise choices in the evening will also help you have time for creation practices the next morning.

Weekly

Taking one day each week to focus *only* on restorative
activities is vital to facing the next week — renewed and
ready for action. This will be a struggle for many, so begin
with a few hours of restoration and see if you can work
your way up to a full day.

Quarterly

Observing a long three-day weekend every few months
gives you some extended time to be restored. It's not quite
the same as a vacation, but certainly more than a normal
weekend.

Periodically

Longer vacations or holiday breaks are on more of a
periodic rhythm, only happening a handful of times each
year.

We tend to ignore the daily, weekly, and quarterly rhythms,
putting all the weight of restoration on that magical vacation.
Unfortunately, a vacation cannot bear that weight. I always joke
that it would be like me eating nothing but pizza and drinking
nothing but scotch for a year, then having salad for a week, and
getting mad that I wasn't skinny at the end of that week. That's
how most people treat rest, but five days of rest can't make up for
360 days of bad habits.

We must honor rest and observe these rhythms to the best
of our ability to put ourselves in the best place to create success.
Sullivan and Hardy describe it this way, "Focus is contraction.
Recovery is expansion."[1] I love the idea that when we are
working, we are focused. Our muscles are contracting and we
are expending our breath. When we rest, our muscles relax, and
our chest expands, filling with air again, restoring us for more
productivity.

From Burnout to Momentum to Sustainable Impact

I said earlier in this chapter that the goal of this book is to put you in a place where you can value yourself enough to prioritize intentional rest as an investment in your success. The tools needed to win the battle against burnout — self-awareness, purpose, and healthy rhythms — will gather dust in the toolbox, unless we believe we are worthy of prioritizing ourselves.

The three elements that keep us trapped in The Burnout Cycle are identity, unsustainable expectations, and judgment. When we reclaim these elements, we can then move into the Momentum Cycle. Here, we are more than willing to get the tools out of the toolbox and use them every day to make sure we show up as healthy leaders. As healthy leaders, we will be able to create Sustainable Impact — the multiplied impact of chasing our purpose with patience and healthy rhythms.

The positive impact we have on ourselves will be multiplied.

The positive impact we have on our families will be multiplied.

The positive impact we have on the entire world will be multiplied.

CHAPTER 16 REFLECTION

Reflection Questions

1. Think of your current life. Do you imagine yourself pushing a boulder alone, or do you embrace teamwork and collaboration?

2. Where are you orienting yourself toward health — spiritually, emotionally, and physically? Where are you off track?

Who do you need in your Circle to support you on the journey?

....

....

....

....

....

....

....

Take Action

1.   Audit your Circle of Support. In what area do you need more people to help you (professional help, mentors, fellow leaders)?

2.   Get out your calendar and intentionally block off time to rest for the remainder of the year. Identify those daily, weekly, quarterly, and vacation times.

CHAPTER 16 ENDNOTES

1. Dan Sullivan and Benjamin Hardy, *10x Is Easier Than 2x: How World-Class Entrepreneurs Achieve More by Doing Less* (Hay House Business, 2023), 185.

"Leadership is
not about being
in charge.
It's about taking
care of those in
your charge."

— Simon Sinek

Chapter 17

SACRED WORK

Burnout is an enemy that will never stop coming after you. This means you have to *choose* to win the battle every day. There will never be a point where you can check the box of healthy leadership and be done. Instead, you must make a daily practice of taking intentional action. *You must choose* how you will lead, and the life you will create, or it will be chosen for you by fear, shame, and burnout.

The first part of that practice is using The Momentum Cycle to ensure you are ready to take care of yourself. Ensure, moment to moment, that you are aligned with the truth of your identity — *you are enough*. Hold yourself accountable to the agreements you have committed to. And use evaluation to measure progress. Using these techniques will set you up to create an impactful life by living as your most authentic self.

Once you are operating from The Momentum Cycle instead of The Burnout Cycle, it's time to deploy the tools to lead sustainably. Embrace self-reflection practices to have a real-time awareness of how you are showing up and being experienced. Use purpose to fuel yourself on your quest for Sustainable Impact. And honor the rhythms necessary to defeat burnout.

Tap into your Circle of Support for help on a regular basis, make intentional choices each moment with Green Light Habits, and find restoration through intentional rest.

Do the work.

It is *sacred* work because it isn't just about us. It's about ensuring that everyone who is "in our care," as Simon Sinek puts it, is taken care of. That includes our families, our teams, our friends, and even ourselves. Our leadership is *sacred*.

If you intentionally and regularly implement the practices in this book, you will create a life that is more impactful and more enjoyable than you can currently imagine. You will create a life that is about purpose, and your legacy will be a positive change in the lives of innumerable people.

Keep Moving Forward

There isn't a day that goes by where I'm not required to use the tools in this book. In fact, I had to use them all just to write the damn thing. I pushed forward, through doubts about my identity (am I truly an author?), questions about my ability (I write words good?), and fear of the judgment of others (yes, I thought about your opinion, dear reader).

In each case, I realigned with the truth of who I am, shed the need to prove anything, embraced my purpose, and pushed forward. When I began this journey with Forward Partners, it was based on a core idea that if we could keep moving forward, we could find whatever success we were looking for.

As you move forward on your journey, doing sacred work, I am right here beside you. I am stumbling, doubting, afraid, and occasionally cursing (sorry, Mom). I am also determined, hopeful, and convinced beyond all evidence that we are going to create an incredible future together.

I leave you with a question from Erwin McManus, from

his book *Mind Shift*: "Do people elevate when they are in the gravitational pull of my life?"

My prayer every day is that this would be true of me — that people would *elevate* when they are in the gravitational pull of my life. I pray the same for you.

Keep moving forward.

FIELD MANUAL

THE BURNOUT CURVE

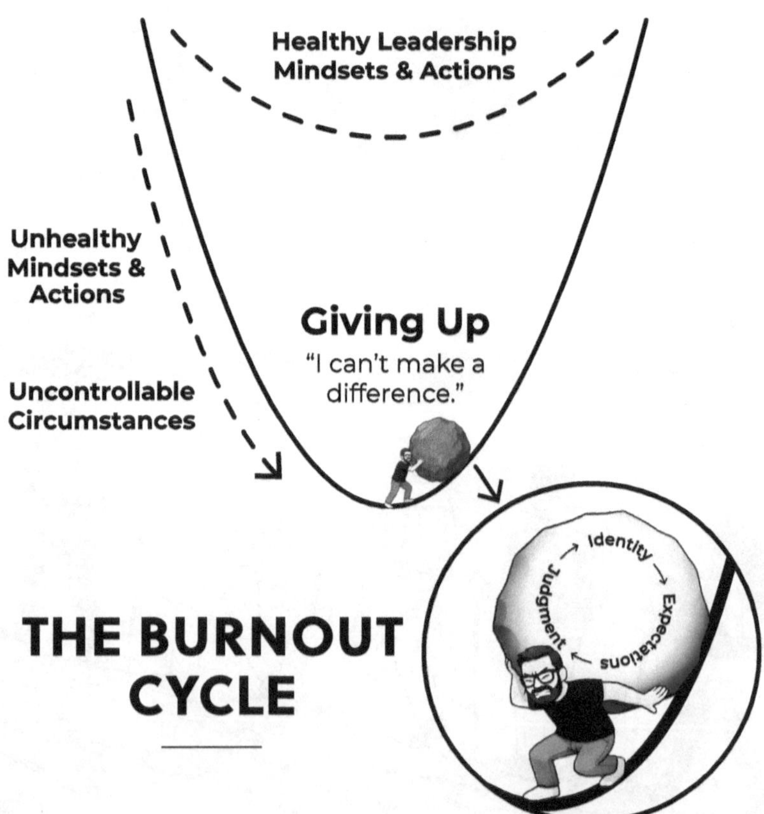

THE BURNOUT CYCLE

RECLAIM THE 3 ELEMENTS

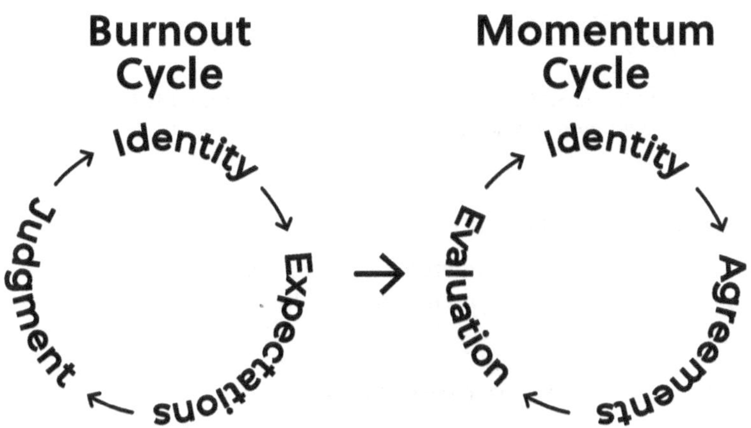

MAKE THE CURVE SHALLOW

Daily Practice

Self-Awareness · Purpose · Rhythms

Circle of Support

Green Light Habits

Intentional Rest Plan

TERMS OF BATTLE

Burnout

Burnout is the loss of capacity to align with your purpose, do your most sacred work, and enjoy life.

Sustainable Impact

Sustainable Impact is the multiplied impact of living your purpose with patience and healthy rhythms.

Unsustainable Expectations

Expectations that are unreasonable, unattainable, unhealthy, or unwanted.

Healthy Leadership

Healthy leaders are spiritually, emotionally, and physically oriented toward health.

CREDITS

Win the Battle Against Burnout:
Reclaim the Three Elements that Trap You in Burnout

Written by Chad Wright

Edited by Elana Jackson

Design by Emily Deal

Illustration by Calla Walshe

Research and Administration by Emily Wright

Video Production and Promotion by Jon Vineyard

Win the Battle Against Burnout was written in Texas, Washington, Oregon, and Colorado. Like everything we do at Forward Partners, it was created with love.

ACKNOWLEDGEMENTS

I would like to start by thanking you. Yes, *you*. I wrote this book for you, and I can't tell you how much it means to me that you would read it. Much love.

For years, I had planned to write a book, but I never knew just how challenging the work would be. I remember when I got serious about planning ahead in 2021. I lined up all the projects we wanted to create, and the book didn't land on the list until 2025. At the time, that seemed like an *eternity* away. In reality, that time flew by, and the book turned into something that I think will be truly impactful — because of that extra time. I honestly can't believe it is finished.

My Forward Partners team is responsible for so much of this project. For years now, Emily Grace Deal has been a creative partner (and partner in podcasting with *The Leader Lab*) and has helped build what Forward Partners is today. Thank you, also, to Emily Wright (yes, we have two Emilys, it's eternally confusing). In addition to being one hell of a director of operations, she's an incredible daughter-in-law. Every day, she keeps me organized and on task, which is no small feat. The two Emilys are the heart of Forward Partners. Thanks to Jon Vineyard for all his assistance over the years in producing our podcasts, and I'm sure a tremendous number of videos to promote this book. To this team, I just want you to know that I love *every second* of our work together, and I can't wait to see where it takes us. I love you all so much.

Thank you to everyone who came before Forward Partners, my Wright Creative Group team (Adam, Aron, Daniel, and Zella).

You walked so we could run. Not a day goes by that I don't laugh at some dumb joke that became part of the office lore.

Terry Ishee, I still miss those long whiteboard sessions we shared when I was beginning to dream of Forward Partners. You asked just the right questions to help me get the crazy thoughts out of my head and onto the whiteboard. Love you, brother.

Thank you, Calla Walshe, for your creative fire and non-stop encouragement. Your illustrations bring this book to life in a really fun way. I know you said you'd like to introduce me some day when I'm receiving a big award, and now I think I'd like to do the same for you!

I deeply appreciate the work of my editor, Elana Jackson. She was encouraging, even through missed deadlines. Like a sculptor, her insight chiseled away the raw edges of this book and revealed the form beneath. Any insight you gleaned from it was shaped by her talents. My ego only occasionally took hits alongside the content — the mark of a great editor.

Thank you to my beta test readers. This book has more clarity and impact thanks to your feedback. Thank you, Alan, Dean, E. A., Elizabeth, Erin, Jared, Kimberly, Mallory, Matthew, Michael, Rachel, Sara, and Scotty.

This book would not be what it is without my work with Becky Henderson. I knew it was time for a new coach to help me solve a very specific problem. Becky was the one to help me solve that, and many other problems since. I remember the first time she told me how much she would charge me. After I was done choking, I started searching the sofa for quarters.

So. Many. Quarters.

What I didn't know at the time was that whatever she charged was *nothing* compared to the life-changing work we would do. Many of the ideas of this book are based on my experience in the trenches, doing *the work*, with Becky. If you are looking to change your life, reach out to her (https://www.plenteouslife.com/).

I also have to call out a man who started as my mentor and

has become an incredible friend — Andrew Tull. (I actually met Becky because of an event that Andrew hosts, proof that finding good mentors can lead to life-changing connections.) I remember when I was introduced to Andrew at a conference. I explained my problem to him and he smiled at me and said, "Good news, that's a solvable problem." Many lunches and a Holiday Party (registered trademark) later, and he is someone I am honored to call a friend and brother. Forward Partners would not be where it is without him.

To Dave Kraft, you were my first coach and a key to the transition from Wright Creative Group to Forward Partners. Your wisdom, insightful questions, and prayers were truly impactful.

I can't think of the early days of Forward Partners without thinking of the Wilco Workspaces extended family. It's a very large group, but much of what exists today was dreamed of in the halls of Wilco Workspaces. That will always be a sacred place to me, and I deeply value the people we connected with there.

Thank you to Tony Moline for his many years of support and deep conversations. VIA313 for life. I obviously can't choose between you and Bridget for my favorite, but she never invites me to VIA, so …

Speaking of Bridget Brandt, I assume you flipped right back here to see if your name made it to the acknowledgements. It did, and was mentioned earlier in the book as well. I'm not telling where; you just have to give it a read. Ever since our first meeting, when I sat in your office and said, "Let me tell you what's *wrong* with the chamber," you've been a great supporter. I'll never forget that Forward Partners launched at a Leander Chamber luncheon.

Thanks to Scotty Crawford for being the newest member of my Circle. As a great spiritual director, he helped me understand how many of my ideas tied to my faith, and how that can impact people of all faiths.

Matthew Wright. My brother from another mother. It started with watches, and now here we are, public service leadership nerds. You're right, it will be hard to convince people that they are enough. Hopefully, this book takes a few steps in that direction.

There is not enough room to thank all of my friends in public service. I have spent the past few years, deep in the trenches with you, deploying the ideas from this book. Much of what is in these pages was first experienced in conference rooms in your city halls. Some of those early, hard-fought lessons involved Emily Crawford, Gina Nash, Lauren Rose, Sereniah Breland, Chief Greg Minton, Chief Mike Harmon, Karen Daly, Kat Caffrey, and so many others. I talk all the time about the *sacred* nature of your work. Keep doing it. We need you. I love you all.

Also on the public service front, thank you to David Morgan from the city of Georgetown, Texas. You invited me to bring the early ideas of this book and beta test them with The Athenian Group. You generously opened many doors for me, and helped solidify the core idea of this book. Thank you to the entire Athenian Group, and a special thanks to Opal Mauldin-Jones. You were the first to challenge me on how these ideas fit with people of various races and backgrounds. I hope this book honors your feedback.

My most sincere apologies to every teacher who had the joy of experiencing me in their class. I'm sure *none* of you believed I'd ever write a book, but you kept pushing me anyway. Thanks for all the extra credit, last-minute makeups, and not challenging my *terrible* lies about why I didn't do my homework. And a special thank-you to Mrs. Sue Gresset. Your impact in my life lasted well beyond the fourth grade. You are truly a saint, just hanging out here on Earth, wearing a TGIF pin. As you say all the time, "God loves you, and so do I."

Thank you, John Veilleux. I'm not sure if you were on a weird detour in life those four years when you decided to teach high school, but you made a difference. And speaking of *The Grass Burr*, well done, David DeGrand. You became a published author before me. I loved *I am Not Okay* and can't wait to read whatever is next.

Thank you, Dr. Mike Vaughn, for your consistent belief in me and investment in my family. You always told me that big things were coming. It just took me a while to be the man who could *create* those things. Thanks for never giving up that belief.

To Dipper, Chris, and O., I love you. Chris, you are an amazing brother. I never knew I needed a second one, but here we are. O., there is no one in this world I like irritating more than you (heart emoji). Dipper, I love you so much. You'll never be chipper, but don't stop trying. With this book, I undoubtedly cement my "golden child" status.

And for my parents, maybe the only people to read *this* far into the book, I honestly don't have the words. You taught me to work hard, which led to a lot of burnout, but then there's my life's work *and* this book, so ... we'll call it good. You modeled for me how to serve others and, most importantly, to *love*. You demonstrate selfless love over and over again. I watch the work you do at the skate park with genuine awe. You have *never* stopped supporting your sons, and you have built a legacy that will impact people generations into the future. I know parents never really feel like they did enough, but just know that you did. I'm proud to call you my parents, and I'll throw hands with anyone who thinks their parents are better. And again, sorry for the cursing, MeeMee, but Dipper says a lot worse.

Speaking of family brings me to Colton, Conner, and Cody. The screen is getting really blurry because, when I think of you, I can't stop the tears from showing up. I am so proud of the men you are. I am often envious of the men you are at *such* young ages. All three of you have the capacity to change the world for everyone around you. Take care of yourselves and continue to serve others every day. Thank you for giving us our first daughters, Emily and Scarlet, and I assume some grandkids someday soon. Also, I'm sure there's a really expensive LEGO set your dad would love to receive to celebrate the launch of this book. Maybe go in together and make that happen. He's earned it.

Finally, thank you to my wife, Rebecca. Babe, as I write this, we are about to celebrate our 25th anniversary. I have given you so *many* reasons to give up. You never have, which speaks to your strength, resilience, and, let's be honest, hard headedness. This book could not have happened if I hadn't burned out so spectacularly. No one endured more pain than you in order for me to learn. The pain has led me to my life's work, and I would not be here without you. You are, and will always be, my lobster, my crouton, my muse, and my best friend. And the sexiest creature I have ever laid eyes on (sorry, kids).

I'm certain I've left a ton of people off this list, and I apologize. It is clear that I am nothing without my community of teachers, friends, team members, and family. If you have read this far, you are *undoubtedly* in that group — and I love you.

Keep Moving Forward,

ABOUT THE AUTHOR

Chad Wright is an author, speaker, facilitator of deep conversations, and amateur philosopher. He and his team at Forward Partners are committed to transforming the future of leadership. He hosts the podcasts *The Leader Lab* and *Leading Thriving Cities*. He could do none of this without an incredible team.

In his off time, he loves nothing more than a good view, a good book, and a good glass of Scotch (or coffee depending on the time of day). He deeply loves his wife Rebecca. They live in Texas, have three adult sons, two daughters-in-law, and a puppy named London.

London is his favorite.

Photograph by Joe Fang

For further leadership development
resources, visit ForwardPartners.net

... or connect with us on LinkedIn.